INNER CLARITY

LET GO OF WHAT HOLDS YOU BACK & STEP INTO WHAT YOU ARE MEANT TO BE

DAVID RIVER

ABSOLUTE AUTHOR PUBLISHING HOUSE

First Edition

Hardback ISBN: 979-8-89401-090-8
Paperback ISBN: 979-8-89401-091-5
eBook ISBN: 979-8-89401-092-2

Library of Congress in Publication Data

Inner Clarity/River, David

1. Self-Help 2. Self-Improvement 3. Self-Growth

PRINTED IN THE UNITED STATES OF AMERICA

About the Author

David River is a writer with a passion for self-discovery, clarity, and personal growth. He believes that lasting change begins within—and that letting go is often the first step toward becoming who we're meant to be.

Inner Clarity was shaped through years of personal reflection, deep thought, and lived experience. Each trait explored in the book was written with honesty and intention, drawing from patterns observed and insights gathered over time. David's writing invites readers inward—with the hope of helping them better understand themselves, grow, and live with greater authenticity.

Dedication

To everyone brave enough to turn inward,

to heal what hurts, and to grow true.

Acknowledgments

There is no journey of growth that happens in isolation.

Though this book was written in moments of deep solitude, it was shaped by countless unseen influences — lessons learned through relationships, challenges & quiet reflections.

To everyone who has crossed my path — whether through kindness, challenge, or inspiration — thank you.

You were part of this transformation, whether you knew it or not.

And to the reader holding this book now: Thank you for your willingness to turn inward, to reflect, to grow.

The journey you are taking is a courageous one. May you continue to walk it with grace, with resilience, and with truth.

Table of Contents

Introduction — Inner Clarity Begins Within

This isn't a book about doing more or being more.

It's about clearing space — releasing what's been quietly weighing you down, and creating room for something deeper to take root.

Before we can grow into who we're meant to be, we have to let go.
Let go of the patterns that keep looping.
Let go of the thoughts that keep us second-guessing ourselves.
Let go of the emotional baggage we've carried for so long, we almost forget it's there.

I wrote this book for anyone who's ever felt stuck — not because they lacked effort, but because they were carrying too much of what no longer fits.

In **Part 1: Letting Go of Inner Burdens**, we'll explore the emotional habits and thought patterns that quietly hold us back.
Some are easy to spot — like anger or resentment.
Others hide behind politeness or fear — like people-pleasing or the need for approval.
But each of them creates distance between us and our real selves.

1

Then, in **Part 2: What to Build Within**, we'll turn the focus toward growth — not quick fixes, but meaningful inner work.

We'll look at the qualities that bring calm, confidence, clarity, and resilience — and how to make them part of who we are.

You don't have to read this book from start to finish.
You don't even need to agree with every word.
But read it slowly. Honestly.
Pause when something makes you uncomfortable.
Linger on the parts that speak to you.

Let this be a gentle mirror — not of your past, but of your potential.

This isn't about chasing perfection.
It's about returning to what's real.
It's about letting go of what no longer fits — and stepping into the life you were meant to live.

PART 1:

LETTING GO OF INNER BURDENS

Part 1 — Letting Go of Inner Burdens

Before we can build within we must first let go of the burdens that no longer serve who we are — or who we are meant to become.

This part of the book is about the negative traits that needs to be uprooted, the emotional habits. the survival patterns, that may have once protected you — but now quietly hinder your growth.

Letting go means freeing yourself from what no longer benefits you.

Each chapter in Part 1 will walk you through a specific trait to let go. You'll explore:
Understand the trait
Why it needs to go
And how to overcome it step by step!

This part will challenge you to be honest — but not harsh. Brave enough to look within — and wise enough to loosen the grip.

This is the inner clearing.
The uprooting The shedding.
The space-making.
The undoing — so the becoming can begin.

Chapter 1: Letting Go of People-Pleasing — From Compliance to Authenticity

"You were not born to please everyone. You were born to be authentic and yourself."

Understanding the Trait

Being kind, helpful, and supportive are beautiful qualities — they build relationships and create harmony. But when these traits are used to **constantly seek approval, avoid rejection, or gain acceptance at the cost of your own needs**, it transforms into something toxic: **people pleasing**.

People pleasers often struggle to say "no," even when something goes against their own values, time, or emotional energy. They fear disappointing others, and they equate self-worth with how well they are liked. But beneath the surface lies an inner conflict — the quiet suppression of their own voice.

> *"When you say 'yes' to others, make sure you're not saying 'no' to yourself."*
>
> *— Paulo Coelho*

Let's be clear:

Being kind doesn't mean being a doormat. Being helpful doesn't mean being hollow. A person can be deeply compassionate while also being clear on what aligns with their values.

What It Looks Like in Real Life

- Saying "yes" even when your heart says "no"

- Feeling guilty for setting healthy boundaries

- Apologizing excessively, even when you've done nothing wrong

- Changing your behavior, appearance, or opinions to win approval

- Feeling anxious if you think someone might be upset with you

Examples You May Recognize

- Taking on extra work or favors because you fear disappointing others

- Going along with group decisions even when you disagree inside

- Feeling responsible for other people's happiness

- Worrying constantly, "What will they think of me?" after a conversation

Why It Needs to Go

People pleasing may look like generosity on the outside, but it often comes with a cost — **resentment, burnout, loss of identity**, and even emotional manipulation. It **dilutes authenticity**, making you a mirror of other people's expectations rather than a reflection of your true self.

> *"You can't live your life for other people. You've got to do what's right for you."*
>
> *– The Notebook*

Over time, people pleasers:

- Compromise their values to avoid conflict

- Struggle with low self-worth

- Feel invisible in relationships

- End up in one-sided, draining dynamics

And the harsh truth?

No matter how much you give, you still won't please everyone.

It's not a goal worth chasing, because it's impossible. What's better? **Being real. Being grounded. Being you.**

How to Overcome It (Step-by-Step)

Step 1: Awareness – Notice Your Patterns

- Ask yourself: Am I doing this because I genuinely want to, or because I fear rejection?

- Reflect on situations where you felt uncomfortable but said "yes" anyway.

- Become mindful of phrases like "I don't mind" or "It's okay" — even when it's not.

  "Awareness is the first step in healing."

  – Dean Ornish

Step 2: Reconnect With Your Core Values

People pleasers often lose touch with what truly matters to them.

- List out your **top 5 personal values** (honesty, respect, authenticity, etc.)

- When a request comes in, ask: Does this align with my values?

- If it doesn't, it's okay to **decline with grace and clarity.**

  "If you don't stand for something, you'll fall for anything."

– Alexander Hamilton

Step 3: Practice Saying No (Without Guilt)

Start small.

- "I really appreciate you thinking of me, but I would have to pass this time."

- "That doesn't work for me right now, but I hope you find what you need." A boundary doesn't need to come with a lengthy explanation. Clarity is kindness.

  "No is a complete sentence."

  – Anne Lamott

Step 4: Build Inner Validation

Instead of feeding off other people's approval, begin validating yourself:

- Journal your achievements and proud moments

- Speak kindly to yourself

- Learn to say, *"I matter too."*

  "You alone are enough. You have nothing to prove to anyone."

  – Maya Angelou

Step 5: Redefine What It Means to Be 'Good'

Being good doesn't mean being available 24/7 or sacrificing your values.

- It means being **honest, balanced, and true**.

- The most respectful relationships are those where both sides **honor each other's boundaries.**

  "Boundaries are the distance at which I can love you and me simultaneously."

  — Prentis Hemphill

Try This Today

Write down one situation where you said "yes" recently but didn't really want to. What could you have said instead that was honest but respectful?

Reflection Prompts

- What do I fear will happen if I say "no"?

- In which relationships do I feel most like a people pleaser?

- What does my ideal, boundary-respecting self look like?

- How would life feel if I lived more honestly and authentically?

- What values do I refuse to compromise on moving forward?

Final Thought to Remember

Being true, real, and authentic — even when it doesn't please everyone — is one of the highest forms of self-respect.

Chapter 2: Letting Go of the Need for Validation — From External Approval to Inner Assurance

"You don't need someone else to tell you that you are enough. You already are."

Understanding the Trait

The desire to feel valued, appreciated, and accepted is part of being human. But when your self-worth starts depending on others' approval, it becomes a silent trap — one that keeps your confidence tied to external sources instead of your own inner compass.

Seeking validation might show up as second guessing your choices, fearing disapproval, or filtering your true self to match what others expect. You may find yourself adjusting your thoughts, actions, and even your personality just to be accepted.

> *"The opinion of others is none of your business."*
>
> *— RuPaul*

At the heart of this pattern is a lack of inner assurance — a shaky relationship with your own voice. When you don't believe in your worth, you start chasing someone else's affirmation to feel whole.

What It Looks Like in Real Life

- Frequently asking others if you're doing the "right thing"

- Feeling unsure or empty without compliments or positive feedback

- Letting others' opinions dictate your self-image

- Believing you're only worthy if you're liked or praised

- Constantly adjusting your words or actions to gain approval

Examples You May Recognize

- Needing praise from a boss, friends, or partner to feel confident in your work

- Checking likes or comments and letting them affect your mood

- Holding back your ideas until you know what others think

- Doubting yourself after even mild criticism or disapproval

Why It Needs to Go

Living for validation makes your emotional state fragile. You're high when praised and low when ignored. Over time, this makes you a passenger in your own life — always seeking signs that you're enough, but never quite arriving there.

Here's what it costs:

- You lose touch with your own values

- You say "yes" when you want to say "no"

- You shrink yourself to avoid disapproval

- You become emotionally drained trying to maintain an image

  "Care about what other people think and you will always be their prisoner."

  — Lao Tzu

True confidence doesn't shout for applause. It stands quietly, rooted in authenticity — whether or not anyone's clapping.

How to Overcome It (Step-by-Step)

Step 1: Know Your Values — Deeply

If you don't know what you stand for, you'll keep bending to you please others.

- List your top 5 personal values (e.g., honesty, creativity, growth, compassion, faith).

- Reflect: Am I living by these values, or by what others expect?

"If you live for people's acceptance, you will die from their rejection."

— *Lecrae Moore*

Step 2: Take Back Your Decisions

Before asking others for input, pause and ask yourself:

- What do I believe is right?

- What choice feels aligned with my truth?

The more you practice this, the more your confidence becomes self-sourced.

Step 3: Be Okay With Being Misunderstood

You don't have to explain every choice or convince every critic.

Not everyone will understand your path — and they don't need to

"Those who mind don't matter, and those who matter don't mind."

— Dr. Seuss

Step 4: Affirm Your Own Worth

Make self-assurance a habit. Remind yourself:

- "I am already enough."

- "My worth isn't dependent on approval."

- "Validation is appreciated, but not required."

Step 5: Break the Social Media Loop

Social media platforms thrive on validation. But you don't have to.

- Don't post for applause.

- Ask: Am I sharing this to connect — or to be seen?

  "The need for approval is the enemy of authenticity."

  — Paul Ferrini

Step 6: Accept That Not Everyone Will Like You

Freedom begins when you stop needing to be liked by all.

The most grounded people aren't everyone's favorite — they're just deeply themselves.

*"You can be the ripest, juiciest peach
in the world, and there's still going to
be someone who hates peaches."*

— Dita Von Teese

Try This Today

Next time you feel the urge to seek validation — pause.

Take a breath.

Ask yourself:
"What would I do if no one else's opinion mattered?"

Then go do exactly that — even if it's just a small step.

Reflection Prompts

- Where in my life do, I constantly seek approval?

- What parts of myself have I changed to fit in?

- What would it feel like to fully trust my own voice?

- Whose validation am I still chasing — and why?

- How can I begin to affirm my own worth, internally?

Final Thought to Remember

You don't need permission to be yourself.
When you stop chasing approval, you finally start living in freedom.

Chapter 3: Letting Go of Fear of Judgment — From Self-Consciousness to Self-Confidence

"Be yourself—everyone else is already taken." – *Oscar Wilde*

Understanding the Trait

Fear of judgment is a quiet yet powerful force. It keeps us from speaking up, taking risks, and being our true selves — all because of one lingering question:
"What will people think of me?"

While it may seem similar to seeking validation, the **core emotion behind fear of judgment is anxiety** — not about being liked, but about being *disapproved of*.
It leads to **self-consciousness**, **emotional hiding**, and often, stagnation.

Comparison: People-Pleasing vs. Validation-Seeking vs. Fear of Judgment

Trait	People-Pleasing	Validation-Seeking	Fear of Judgment
Core Desire	Keeping others happy and avoiding conflict	Craving approval and praise	Avoiding criticism, shame, or rejection
Motivation	"Please don't be upset with me"	"Please like me"	"Please don't reject me"
Behavior	Saying yes, over-accommodating, self-neglect	Performing to gain attention or applause	Shrinking or hiding to avoid negativity
Underlying Emotion	Guilt, fear of disapproval, low boundaries	Insecurity & need for worth	Anxiety & fear of exposure
How it shows up	Agreeing too quickly, avoiding disagreement	Over-sharing, seeking spotlight	Holding back, self-censoring
Result	Exhaustion, loss of self	Exhaustion from performing	Regret from not showing up at all

People-pleasing says: 'Please don't be upset with me.'
Seeking validation says: 'I want you to accept me.'
Fear of judgment says: 'I fear you'll reject me.'

What It Looks Like in Real Life

- Staying silent in meetings or social settings even when you have something to contribute

- Holding back your true personality, creativity, or emotions

- Overthinking your words, appearance, or presence

- Avoiding opportunities, leadership roles, or expressing unpopular opinions

- Feeling physically anxious or mentally frozen in fear of "being seen the wrong way"

Examples You May Recognize

- A student who knows the answer in class, but won't raise their hand for fear of being wrong

- An artist who hides their work because someone once laughed at their drawing

- A professional who avoids public speaking or video calls because they're afraid of being judged for how they sound or look

- A young person who stifles their personality online because they fear trolls, mockery, or being "cancelled"

"Stop shrinking to fit places you've outgrown."

Why It Needs to Go

Fear of judgment is one of the biggest barriers to personal freedom. It trains you to live from the outside in — constantly adjusting, filtering, and holding back your light. And over time, it convinces you that **your real self is unsafe to show**.

Here's what it slowly steals:

- Your voice

- Your dreams

- Your authenticity

- Your potential

- Your ability to live without apology

"You don't owe the world a perfect version of you. You owe it a real one."

The truth is — people will judge you no matter what. The question is: ***Will you betray yourself just to avoid their opinion?***

How to Overcome It (Step-by-Step)

Step 1: Acknowledge the Fear Without Shame

Admit it kindly: *"I'm afraid of being judged."* This is a human fear — but it doesn't have to be your identity. The moment you name it, you weaken its grip.

Step 2: Identify Your "Audience"

Who are you most afraid of being judged by?

- Parents? Strangers? Social media? Coworkers?

Ask yourself:

- *"Have they really earned the power I've given them?"*

- *"Am I sacrificing my truth for their approval or silence?"*

Step 3: Reclaim Your Right to Be Seen

You have the right to speak, to express, to exist fully.

Try saying:

- *"I don't have to be perfect to be present."*

- *"My opinion is valid."*

- *"It's safe for me to be seen."*

Confidence doesn't mean having no fear. It means choosing **truth over safety**.

"If you avoid being seen, you also avoid being understood."

Step 4: Start Showing Up in Small Ways

Courage is built in micro-steps:

- Share your idea, even if your voice shakes

- Post your art or writing

- Wear the outfit that expresses you

- Say what you believe in — kindly but clearly

The more you do it, the less fearful it feels.

"The cure for fear of judgment is exposure — not avoidance."

Step 5: Shift From Self-Consciousness to Self-Compassion

When fear arises, don't attack yourself. Support yourself.

Instead of:

- *"They're judging me."* Say:

- *"I'm doing something brave."*

- *"Even if someone dislikes it, I know I'm growing."*

Let self-compassion drown out imagined criticism.

Try This Today

Write down one thing you've held back from doing because of fear of judgment.
Now ask:

- *What's the worst that could realistically happen?*

- *What could open up for me if I did it anyway?*

Take one bold step toward it — even a small one.

Reflection Prompts

- What's one area of my life where I constantly censor or shrink myself?

- Whose opinions have I given too much weight — and why?

- How would my life change if I stopped worrying about being *"too much"* or *"not enough"*?

- What does it feel like to accept myself more than I fear others?

- What part of me am I ready to let the world see?

Final Thought to Remember

You were not created to be invisible. Let them judge — and keep shining anyway.

Chapter 4: Letting Go of the Need for Attention — From Spotlight Seeking to Inner Fulfillment

"People who shine from within don't need the spotlight." — Unknown

Understanding the Trait

The desire to be seen, heard, and acknowledged is deeply human. We all want to feel significant. But when the **need for attention** becomes a driving force — when your actions revolve around gaining recognition, sympathy, admiration, or applause — it begins to erode your authenticity.

Attention-seeking isn't always loud or dramatic. It can show up subtly:

- Oversharing struggles to gain sympathy

- Bragging about achievements for admiration

- Constant social media posting for approval

- Making yourself the center of conversations

- Using humor, sarcasm, or drama to stay noticed

"Some people create drama because it's the only way they know to be noticed."

— Steve Maraboli

What often lies beneath this need is a deeper emotional void — **a lack of internal validation**, fear of being invisible, or a belief that you need to be "extra" to be worthy.

What It Looks Like in Real Life

- Feeling uncomfortable or restless when not the center of attention

- Sharing personal stories mainly to gain sympathy or admiration

- Feeling validated only when others notice, praise, or applaud you

- Craving external recognition for achievements or even small actions

- Becoming discouraged if your efforts go unnoticed

Examples You May Recognize

- Exaggerating your successes to impress others

- Feeling irritated or overlooked when conversations aren't about you

- Seeking sympathy through frequent sharing of struggles, not for support, but for attention

- Showing off possessions, achievements, or experiences primarily to gain admiration

- Feeling unseen or unworthy if you're not regularly praised or spotlighted

Why It Needs to Go

The need for constant attention turns your life into a performance. Instead of living from the inside out — rooted in your values and truth — you live from the outside in, adjusting yourself to whatever gets the most reaction.

Here's what it costs:

- You develop **shallow relationships** that are based on entertainment, not connection.

- You feel **emotionally drained** trying to maintain the spotlight.

- You lose sight of your true identity.

- You become **dependent on external stimulation** to feel valuable.

- You confuse validation with love.

  "Don't trade your authenticity for approval."

Even empathy-seeking can be a form of attention seeking — when people share their pain primarily to be the center of sympathy, rather than for healing or connection. While vulnerability is powerful, using it as a tool to stay relevant can keep you stuck in victimhood instead of growth.

How to Overcome It (Step-by-Step)

Step 1: Build Awareness — What Am I Really Needing?

Attention-seeking usually masks another emotional need — to be valued, to feel important, to feel loved.

- Ask yourself: What am I truly craving right now? Connection? Validation? Significance?

- Name the deeper emotion underneath your behavior.

    "The quieter you become, the more you can hear."

    – *Ram Dass*

Step 2: Redirect From Performance to Presence

You don't need to perform to be seen. You just need to be present.

- Practice listening more than speaking in conversations.

- Show up fully instead of trying to steal the spotlight.

- Let your value be felt, not flaunted.

Step 3: Resist the Urge to Overshare for Sympathy or Applause

Before sharing a struggle or success, ask:

- Am I sharing to connect or to impress?

- Am I looking for support or attention?

Authenticity is quiet. You can share without dramatizing. You can be vulnerable without needing pity.

Step 4: Quiet Confidence Over Loud Validation

Real strength doesn't need to announce itself.

- Focus on doing meaningful things — not for praise, but for purpose.

- When you do well, let your satisfaction come from within, not from reactions.

  "Work hard in silence. Let success make the noise."

  — Frank Ocean

Step 5: Step Away From the Spotlight (On Purpose)

Intentionally give others the space to shine.

- Compliment someone else.

- Ask someone their story.

- Let others speak while you listen fully.

You'll be surprised how valued you feel simply by creating value around you.

Step 6: Find Fulfillment in Solitude

Attention-seeking thrives when you can't sit with yourself.

- Spend time in silence.

- Go on solo walks, journal, or simply sit in quiet reflection.

- Learn to be okay without anyone watching, clapping, or reacting.

    "Learn to be alone and to like it. There's nothing more freeing."

    – Mandy Hale

Try This Today

Go through a whole day without trying to draw attention to yourself — no interrupting, no one upping, no over-posting, no humblebragging.

Instead, focus on making others feel seen. Observe how that shifts your energy.

Reflection Prompts

- In what areas of life do I find myself seeking attention the most?

- What deeper emotion or insecurity is driving this need?

- How do I behave when I feel unnoticed or unappreciated?

- What would it look like to be secure in my presence — even when I'm not in the spotlight?

- How can I serve or support others without needing recognition?

Final Thought to Remember

You don't need attention to be valuable. You were enough even before anyone noticed you.

Chapter 5: Letting Go of Herd Mentality — From Blind Following to Independent Thinking

"The opposite of courage in our society is not cowardice. It is conformity." – Rollo May

Understanding the Trait

Herd mentality happens when we follow the crowd without questioning where it's going — or why we're even following in the first place. It's when you adopt opinions, behaviors, or beliefs just because everyone else seems to be doing it.

In a world full of trends, noise, and social pressure, standing still or stepping aside can feel almost unnatural. But that's exactly what herd mentality preys on: our deep need to fit in, to feel safe, to avoid conflict or judgment.

At its core, it's not just about going along with others. It's about abandoning our own voice in the process.

> *"The greatest prison people live in is the fear of what others think."*
>
> *— David Icke*

What It Looks Like in Real Life

- Repeating opinions without researching or understanding them

- Following trends or popular opinions even when they clash with your values

- Staying silent in a group, even when you disagree

- Making choices based on popularity, not principle

- Feeling uneasy when you stand out — and relieved when you blend in

Examples You May Recognize

- Sharing an opinion on social media just because it's trending

- Going along with group behavior, even when your gut says it's wrong

- Changing your mind just to avoid being the "odd one out"

- Defending something publicly that you privately question

- Avoiding personal goals because they don't match what others expect

Why It Needs to Go

When you live by herd mentality, you shrink your individuality. You don't get to know what you truly believe, because you're too busy echoing the voices around you.

Over time, this leads to:

- Regret over choices made to please others

- Confusion about your real identity or values

- Missed opportunities that required risk or standing alone

- A quiet resentment for not being true to yourself

    "Don't be satisfied with stories, how things have gone with others. Unfold your own myth."

    – Rumi

Letting go of herd mentality doesn't mean rejecting others — it means reclaiming your ability to think, feel, and act from a place of clarity and conviction.

How to Overcome It (Step-by-Step)

Step 1: Question the Crowd

When you catch yourself following along, ask:

- "Do I actually believe this?"

- "Would I still choose this if no one else was watching?"

Curiosity is the first sign of independence.

Step 2: Get Clear on Your Own Values

Write down your personal values — not the ones you were taught to repeat, but the ones that feel true to you.
Let them become your compass.

> *"In a world that profits from your distraction, clarity is a rebellion."*
>
> *— Unknown*

Step 3: Practice Micro-Courage

You don't need to start by shouting unpopular truths. Start small:

- Share a different opinion calmly

- Make a choice that aligns with your goals, even if others don't get it

- Say "no" without guilt when something doesn't feel right

Step 4: Embrace Discomfort

Standing alone can feel awkward — but it's often a sign you're finally standing in your truth. Discomfort isn't danger. It's growth.

Step 5: Surround Yourself with Thinkers, Not Echoes

Seek out people who encourage dialogue, not just agreement. Read, reflect, and expose yourself to different perspectives — not to adopt them blindly, but to sharpen your own.

Try This Today

Think of one belief or decision you've been going along with — not because you believe it, but because it's easier.

Pause. Reevaluate.

Then take one small step that reflects your own voice — not the crowd's.

Reflection Prompts

- Where in my life am I blending in at the cost of being real?

- What's one opinion I've repeated without truly exploring it?

- How does it feel when I stand alone in a belief or decision?

- Who in my life encourages my independence — and who pressures conformity?

- What would it look like to choose authenticity over approval?

Final Thought to Remember

The loudest voices aren't always the wisest. Let your life be guided not by the crowd — but by the quiet conviction of your own inner compass.

Chapter 6: Letting Go of Ego — From Arrogance to Authentic Confidence

"Pride makes us artificial; humility makes us real." – Thomas Merton

Understanding the Trait

Ego has many faces: arrogance, boastfulness, superiority complexes, extreme self-centeredness — and sometimes, a quiet sense of being better than others.

It tells us we have to prove ourselves, compete for attention, and protect our image — even if it costs us authenticity, humility, and real connection.

At its core, ego is insecurity disguised as confidence.
When we don't feel enough on the inside, we try to look more than enough on the outside.

Let's explore how ego can take shape:

- **Arrogance**

Arrogance tells you you're always right. It blocks feedback, resists correction, and assumes there's nothing left to learn. The arrogant person talks more than they listen — and listens only to respond, not to understand.

"Arrogance is the camouflage of insecurity."

– Tim Fargo

- **Boastfulness**

Boastfulness feeds off recognition. It needs to be seen, praised, and admired. It shows up in constant self-promotion — whether about money, accomplishments, looks, or knowledge.

"Let someone else praise you, not your own mouth."

– Unknown

- **Haughtiness**

Haughtiness carries subtle contempt. It's the tone, the lifted chin, the dismissive glance. It whispers, "I'm above you," and thrives on comparison

"A proud man is always looking down on things and people; and, of course, as long as you're looking down, you can't see something that's above you."

– C.S. Lewis

- **Extreme self-centeredness**

This centers everything around the self. It demands attention, avoids vulnerability, and treats people like props for admiration.

"Ego is just an unhealthy belief in your own importance."

– Ryan Holiday

- **Superiority Complex**

This is ego in its most deceptive form — the belief that you're inherently better than others. It doesn't always show through words — sometimes, it hides in quiet judgment.
Examples include:

- Feeling intellectually superior

- Believing your lifestyle or choices are the "right" way

- Looking down on others for their job, background, or appearance

"The moment you think you're better than someone is the moment you've stopped growing."

This mindset disconnects you from empathy, humility — and your own humanity.

What It Looks Like in Real Life

- Always needing to be "right" in arguments

- Feeling superior based on success, intelligence, or appearance

- Dismissing others' ideas without consideration

- Taking offense when your status isn't acknowledged

- Struggling to apologize or admit you're wrong

Examples You May Recognize

- Correcting someone sharply just to prove a point

- Feeling secretly pleased when others fail

- Thinking, "I could do that better" — without trying

- Becoming defensive when receiving feedback

- Needing to "win" in social comparisons

How Each Trait Is Different

Trait	Root Emotion	Focus	How It Shows
Arrogance	Insecurity + control	Being right	Dismisses feedback, dominates conversations
Boastfulness	Insecurity + need for praise	Being admired	Bragging, self-centered storytelling
Haughtiness	Fear of inferiority	Social elevation	Coldness, subtle contempt, judgmental tone
Extreme Self Centeredness	Emptiness + entitlement	Self-centered validation	Lacks empathy, manipulates attention
Superiority Complex	Insecurity + comparison	Feeling "above" others	Silent or subtle judgment of others

Identifying how ego shows up is the first step toward real transformation — from trying to impress to showing up with authenticity.

Why It Needs to Go

Ego might offer a moment of satisfaction, but it costs you deeply:

- **Growth** — You resist feedback and stop evolving

- **Connection** — Others feel judged, not understood

- **Peace** — You're always comparing, performing, or proving

- **Respect** — True respect is earned, not demanded

  "You can have either pride or peace — never both."

  – Unknown

Letting go of ego brings clarity, humility, deeper relationships — and confidence that doesn't need applause.

How to Overcome It (Step-by-Step)

Step 1: Notice Where Ego Shows Up

- Do you feel irritated when someone else is right?

- Do you compare your lifestyle or success?

- Do you dismiss others to feel more secure?

Just notice. No shame — only awareness.

"Awareness is the birthplace of transformation."

Step 2: Replace Superiority With Empathy

Instead of thinking "I'm better", think "We're all human."

- Pause before judging someone's choices or struggles.

- Remind yourself someone else's value doesn't threaten yours.

   "Be kind, for everyone you meet is fighting a battle you know nothing about."

   — Wendy Mass

Step 3: Practice Humble Confidence

Humility isn't weakness — it's grounded strength.

- Speak when needed, not to impress.

- Know your worth without needing to broadcast it.

- Be open to learning from anyone.

   "True humility is not thinking less of yourself, but thinking of yourself less."

Step 4: Let Go of the Need to Be Right

Ego argues. Confidence listens.

- Ask yourself: "Am I here to connect — or to win?"

- Give others space to express themselves fully.

  "It is the mark of an educated mind to be able to entertain a thought without accepting it."

  – Aristotle

Step 5: Step Away From Performance

You don't have to prove your success.

- Let your presence speak louder than your stories.

- Do well even when no one is watching.

  "The real measure of success is how quietly you carry it."

  – Unknown

Step 6: Invite Vulnerability

Ego hides flaws. Confidence embraces them.

- Say "I don't know" without shame.

- Apologize sincerely when you're wrong.

- Ask for help when needed.

"There is nothing more attractive than humility that doesn't need a spotlight."

Try This Today

Next time you feel the urge to impress, compare, or correct — pause.
Let someone else speak first. Celebrate their win.
Stay grounded in your worth.

Reflection Prompts

- In what ways do I try to seem superior — even subtly?

- How would it feel to stop needing to impress people?

- What do I fear would happen if I admitted I was wrong?

- How do I treat those I perceive as "less than" me?

- What would humility look like in my words and actions this week?

Final Thought to Remember

You don't need to be above anyone — just aligned with who you truly are.
Confidence is quiet. Ego is just noise.

Chapter 7: Letting Go of Inferiority — Balancing Self-Worth Without Superiority

"No one can make you feel inferior without your consent." — Eleanor Roosevelt

Understanding the Trait

In the previous chapter, we explored the inflated side of the ego — superiority, arrogance, boastfulness, and the illusion of being above others. Now, we shift to its quieter counterpart: **inferiority** — the deeply rooted belief that you are **less than, unworthy**, or **not enough** in comparison to others.

Unlike arrogance, inferiority is rarely loud. It hides in silence, in self-doubt, in the shrinking of your voice and presence. It shows up as:

- Believing others are more capable, valuable, or deserving than you

- Feeling like you don't belong or that you're always behind

- Measuring your worth by status, appearance, approval, or productivity

- Avoiding opportunities out of fear you're not "good enough"

"Inferiority doesn't always scream — sometimes it simply tells you to stay quiet and stay small."

And while superiority pushes others down, inferiority **pushes you down**. It convinces you that your place is beneath others — in thought, value, or existence.

Yet both superiority and inferiority stem from the same root: **a distorted view of self-worth shaped by comparison.**

"Superiority and inferiority are two sides of the same illusion. When you let go of both, you begin to walk in true self-respect — where no one is greater, and no one is lesser."

What It Looks Like in Real Life

- Constantly comparing yourself to others and feeling like you fall short

- Undermining or dismissing your own accomplishments

- Staying silent in conversations, assuming your input doesn't matter

- Thinking, "Why would anyone care what I think?"

- Feeling out of place, even when you're fully qualified or welcomed

Examples You May Recognize

- A woman who never shares her ideas at work because she believes others are more experienced

- A man who avoids social situations because he feels like he doesn't "measure up"

- A student who won't apply for a scholarship because they assume someone else is more deserving

- A person who downplays their talents, beauty, or kindness — afraid to be seen

"You are not too little. You are not too late. You are not less."

Why It Needs to Go

Inferiority may seem like a harmless emotion — even mistaken for humility. But it slowly erodes your confidence, potential, and joy.

It teaches you to:

- Settle for less

- Stay in the background

- Diminish your voice

- Hide your strengths

- Overvalue others while undervaluing yourself

But true humility isn't about thinking less of yourself — it's about seeing yourself clearly. It means recognizing your strengths, owning your weaknesses, and growing through both.

How to Overcome It (Step-by-Step)

Step 1: Catch the Comparison Thought

Inferiority thrives in comparison. Begin noticing when your mind says:

- "They're better than me."

- "I could never do what they do."

- "I don't belong here."

Interrupt the thought gently and ask:

"Is this a fact — or a fear?"

Step 2: Reclaim the Inner Balance

Remind yourself:

- "I'm not above anyone — and I'm not beneath anyone."

- "I have my own path, gifts, and pace."

- "Their success is not my failure."

This isn't about false confidence — it's about inner balance.

Step 3: Affirm Your Unique Value

Your worth isn't based on:

- Your job title

- Your appearance

- Your follower count

- How you compare to others

Your worth is inherent. It exists because you exist.

"Confidence doesn't mean thinking you're better. It means knowing you don't have to be."

Step 4: Take Up Your Space, Bit by Bit

Say what you genuinely think in conversations — not to impress, but to express.
Accept compliments without deflecting.
Show up for the opportunity even if you're unsure.
Try, speak, apply, share.

Don't wait until you feel "ready" to be worthy — your worth comes first.

Step 5: Surround Yourself with What Lifts You

Limit time with people, media, or environments that fuel feelings of inferiority.

Instead, choose:

- People who celebrate you, not compete with you

- Voices that empower, not compare

- Environments where you feel safe to grow

You are allowed to protect your confidence while it's healing.

Try This Today

Write down five qualities you admire in others.
Then write how you already embody — or can begin to develop — each one.

Let it be a reminder that you're not behind — you're becoming.

Reflection Prompts

- Where in my life do I feel "less than" others — and why?

- What past experiences may have shaped this belief?

- Do I confuse humility with low self-worth?

- How do I behave when I feel inferior — and how does it affect my choices?

- What would it feel like to stand equal with others — not above, not below?

Final Thought to Remember

You are not better than others. And you are not beneath them. True self-worth and confidence live in the middle — quiet, steady, and unshaken by comparison.

Chapter 8: Letting Go of Double Standards — From Inconsistency to Integrity

"Justice is not only about doing right, but doing it equally." — Unknown

Understanding the Trait

Double standards show up when we apply one set of rules to ourselves — or to a specific group — and another set to everyone else. They create invisible lines of inequality in how we judge, excuse, forgive, or criticize behavior.

They can be subtle or blatant. Sometimes, they emerge internally:

- We justify our own mistakes but harshly judge others for similar ones.

- We expect understanding for our circumstances but refuse to extend the same grace to others.

Other times, double standards appear in how we treat people based on status, gender, background, or power:

- A wealthy or influential person is given the benefit of the doubt, while someone from a marginalized or lower-status group is quickly condemned.

- A friend is forgiven, but a stranger is punished for the same misstep.

- Someone's success is celebrated, while the same success in someone else is questioned or downplayed.

"We judge ourselves by our intentions and others by their actions."

– Stephen R. Covey

This inconsistency is not just unfair — it damages trust, distorts truth, and erodes our integrity.

What It Looks Like in Real Life

- Criticizing others for behaviors you excuse in yourself

- Expecting loyalty but not offering it

- Treating those in power more favorably than those without it

- Letting someone you like get away with something, but holding a grudge when someone else does it

- Making excuses for a loved one's mistakes, but demanding perfection from strangers

Examples You May Recognize

- Thinking, "I was just having a bad day" — but assuming someone else is rude by nature

- Letting a popular or respected figure slide for saying something hurtful, but harshly criticizing someone less known for the same

- Expecting patience when you're late, but being annoyed when others are

- Defending someone who hurt others because they're "not usually like that," but never extending the same compassion elsewhere

Why It Needs to Go

Double standards fracture fairness. They create emotional distance and damage credibility — in both personal and social relationships.

Here's what it costs:

- **Trust:** People see through inconsistency. Over time, it makes your words feel empty.

- **Respect:** Favoritism and hypocrisy diminish respect — both the kind you receive and the kind you give.

- **Self-Alignment:** You can't feel truly at peace if your values are bent depending on who you're dealing with.

   "You can't demand honesty from others if you're not honest with yourself."

   — Unknown

Letting go of double standards is not just about fairness —
it's about freedom. It frees you from the burden of
justifying inconsistencies and allows you to live in
alignment with truth.

How to Overcome It (Step-by-Step)

Step 1: Call Out the Inconsistency

Notice when you catch yourself judging someone else
harshly but letting yourself — or others — off the hook.
Ask:

- "Would I feel the same if the roles were reversed?"

- "Am I giving myself more benefit of the doubt than
  I give others?"

Step 2: Hold Yourself to the Same Standards You Expect

Before correcting someone else,
Ask:

- *"Am I living by the same standard?"*
  This doesn't mean being harsh with yourself — it
  means being honest.

Step 3: Practice Equal Compassion and Accountability

Don't only show kindness to people you like or agree with.
Ask:

- *"Would I give this person grace if they were a loved one?"*

- *"Am I willing to hold those I admire accountable, too?"*

"Fairness is not about treating everyone the same. It's about being consistent with your values."

— Unknown

Step 4: Reflect on Status Bias

Do you treat people differently based on title, wealth, looks, or popularity?
If someone with less influence made the same mistake — would you react the same way?
Challenge yourself to see the person, not the position.

Step 5: Speak and Act With Integrity

Let your standards be clear — and universal.
When you live by principles instead of preferences, you become someone others trust, and someone you respect.

Try This Today

Choose one recent moment when you held someone to a harsher standard than you'd hold yourself — or vice versa.
Ask:

- What would fairness look like here?

- How can I approach this situation with integrity instead of bias?

Then, take one small action that reflects that shift.

Reflection Prompts

- Where in my life do I apply double standards — even unintentionally?

- Do I excuse behavior in myself that I judge in others?

- How do I treat people differently based on status, likeability, or familiarity?

- What would consistency in values look like in my words and actions?

- How can I practice fairness without losing compassion?

Final Thought to Remember

Let your values lead — not your preferences, your biases, or your mood. When you live without double standards, you walk in clarity, fairness, and true inner strength.

Chapter 9: Letting Go of Entitlement — From Expectation to Empowerment

"You are not owed anything by the world. Everything is a gift, not a guarantee." –Unknown

Understanding the Trait

Entitlement is the belief that you are owed something — by life, by people, by circumstances — simply because you exist, because you've suffered, or because you think you deserve it. It may not always be voiced, but it lives in the background of thoughts like:

- "I should be treated better."

- "I deserve this just because I want it."

- "They should've known what I needed."

- "Life should give me what I expect."

Entitlement doesn't always sound demanding. Sometimes, it shows up as quiet frustration, comparison, or bitterness.

> *"Expectations feed frustration. It is an unhealthy attachment to people,*

*things, and outcomes we wish we
could control."*

– Steve Maraboli

Where Entitlement Comes From:

- **Overindulgence or childhood conditioning:**
  If someone has always been given what they want,
  they may struggle when life says "no."

- **Comparison with others:** Seeing people succeed and
  thinking *"I deserve that too"* — without acknowledging
  their effort or path.

- **Unprocessed pain:** Believing that because you've
  suffered, the world now owes you something better.

- **Inflated ego:** Assuming superiority in worth or
  intelligence, and expecting the world to align
  accordingly.

The Emotional Cost of Entitlement:

- **Chronic frustration** — because things rarely go
  exactly as imagined

- **Resentment in relationships** — when people
  don't meet your silent expectations

- **Stagnation** — because waiting to be given
  something kills the drive to earn or grow

- **Lack of gratitude** — because the focus is always
  on what's missing, not what's present

- **Victim mindset** — believing life is unfair and others are to blame

Entitlement traps you in a cycle of expectation and disappointment.

But when you let go of it, you make room for something better: **empowerment.**

What It Looks Like in Real Life

- Believing you deserve special treatment without corresponding effort

- Feeling resentful when things don't go your way

- Expecting others to meet your needs without clearly communicating them

- Thinking rules, inconveniences, or sacrifices should apply to others — not to you

- Feeling easily offended when reality doesn't match your expectations

Examples You May Recognize

- Feeling frustrated when success doesn't come quickly, despite little action

- Believing you deserve a promotion, relationship, or reward without putting in the necessary effort

- Resenting others' success as unfair instead of recognizing their hard work

- Expecting others to prioritize your needs or accommodate your feelings automatically

- Feeling slighted if you don't receive attention, praise, or help without asking

Why It Needs to Go

Entitlement might feel like self-respect, but it's really emotional dependency. It says, *"My happiness depends on how others treat me and what life gives me."*

The problem?

- People don't always behave how you expect.

- Life doesn't always follow your script.

- And the longer you wait for fairness, the more you'll resent reality.

Letting go of entitlement doesn't mean accepting less. It means owning your path.
It means replacing passive expectation with active responsibility.

> *"Don't wish it were easier. Wish you were better."*
>
> – *Jim Rohn*

How to Overcome It (Step-by-Step)

Step 1: Identify Where You Feel Owed

Ask yourself honestly:

- *"Do I expect others to know what I need without asking?"*

- *"Do I feel resentful when life doesn't go as planned?"*

- *"Do I often think "I deserve better" without working toward it?"*

Write down these areas. Becoming aware is the first step to release.

Step 2: Reframe "Deserve" Into "Earn" or "Grow Toward"

Entitlement thrives on the belief that we should automatically receive certain things — success, happiness, validation, or respect — without self-awareness or growth.

Instead of saying *"I deserve respect,"* try asking:

- *"Am I living in a way that invites respect?"*

- *"Am I respecting others the way I want to be respected?"*

Demanding respect is often a subtle form of entitlement — especially when it's expected without offering respect in return, or when it's tied to status, age, or ego. True respect can't be forced. It flows from character, humility, and how we treat others, even when we disagree.

"You can't force people to respect you, but you can live in a way that makes it impossible not to."

When you shift from *"I deserve"* to *"I'll become,"* you move from waiting to creating.
From frustration to empowerment.

"Success isn't something you deserve. It's something you develop."

Step 3: Replace Expectation With Gratitude

Gratitude dissolves entitlement. It focuses on what is, not what's missing.

- Start a daily gratitude practice.

- Say "thank you" more often .

- Acknowledge small blessings as much as big ones.

  "He who is not grateful for a little, will not be grateful for much."

  — Prophet Muhammad (Peace be upon Him)- Prophet of Islam

Step 4: Take Full Responsibility For Your Life

Entitlement waits. Responsibility acts.

- If something is lacking, ask: *"What can I do?"*

- Replace blame with ownership.

- Don't wait for things to change — *become the change.*

"Responsibility is the price of freedom."

— Elbert Hubbard

Try This Today

Think of something you're frustrated about.
Now ask yourself:

- *"Was I expecting something to happen for me?"*

- *"What can I actively do instead?"*

Write down one empowering action you can take — and do it today.

Reflection Prompts

- Where in my life do I feel I'm owed something — and why?

- How does entitlement affect my relationships or emotional peace?

- What would it feel like to release expectation and embrace action?

- What am I grateful for right now, that I used to take for granted?

- How can I trade blame for responsibility in one area of my life?

Final Thought to Remember

You're not owed an easier life — but you're capable of building a stronger one. Let go of what you expect, and grow into what you create.

Chapter 10: Letting Go of Negative Thinking — From Negative Filters to Clear Vision

"The way you see others is a reflection of what you've yet to see in yourself." — Unknown

Understanding the Trait

Negative thinking isn't just about having a bad day — it's a mental habit. A pattern that can subtly color the way you see people, situations, and even yourself. It often shows up as criticism, pessimism, judgment, or quietly hoping others fall short. But one of the most impactful forms of negative thinking is **projection** — when we unconsciously assign our own difficult emotions or behaviors to someone else.

Often, we're not truly describing other people — we're unknowingly revealing parts of ourselves.

> *"We don't see things as they are. We see them as we are."*
>
> *— Anaïs Nin*

What Is Projection, Really?

71

Projection is a defense mechanism — the mind's way of avoiding discomfort by deflecting it outward.

Rather than acknowledging a difficult emotion, we pin it on someone else.

It's like holding up a mirror to the world and mistaking the reflection for reality.

"The world is your mirror — what you see in others is often what lies within you."

— Unknown

What It Looks Like in Real Life

- You find yourself pointing out what's wrong in others, even when you haven't reflected on your own behavior.

- You assume people are being fake, manipulative, or unkind — without any clear reason why.

- You get especially irritated by certain traits in others... because deep down, you struggle with those same things.

- You make sarcastic or cynical comments, not realizing they might be covering up something more vulnerable underneath.

- You quickly label someone as arrogant or selfish, even though you don't really know them well.

- You catch yourself rolling your eyes at someone's happiness or success — not because they did anything wrong, but because it stirred something unsettled in you.

- You feel a strong urge to correct, critique, or call people out — without pausing to ask what part of that frustration might actually be yours.

Examples You May Recognize:

- Someone who secretly feels jealous might accuse another of being envious:

  "Why are YOU so jealous all the time?"

- A person who often lies might say:

  "I don't trust you — you're probably lying."

In both cases, they're projecting their own unresolved feelings outward.

> *"What we judge in others often reveals the battles we hide within ourselves."*
>
> *— Unknown*

Your perception of others is a reflection of yourself.

When you look at others, you're often seeing parts of yourself.

If you constantly label people as rude, selfish, or fake — it's worth asking:

Is this about them? Or something unresolved in me?

How you interpret others says a lot about your inner world.

> **"When your heart is cloudy, even the purest souls look stained."**
>
> *— Unknown*

Other Forms of Negative Thinking That Hold You Back

It's not always projection. Sometimes, negative thinking comes in other shapes:

- **Pessimism** — assuming the worst before it happens

  "Nothing ever works out."

- **Harsh judgment** — measuring others with moral superiority *"I'd never do what they did."*

- **Schadenfreude** — feeling satisfied when others fail

  "Good — now they know how it feels."

These thoughts might feel like protection, but they create emotional distance — from others, and from your own joy.

How It Feels Internally

- Emotionally drained, tense, or bitter

- Constantly suspicious or guarded

- Struggling to trust or celebrate others

- Comparing yourself often

- Expecting disappointment before it even happens

  "You can't live a positive life with a negative mind."

  – Joyce Meyer

What It Looks Like in Real Life

- Highlighting what's wrong instead of what's right

- Assuming people have hidden motives

- Judging yourself or others for small things

- Focusing on problems instead of possibilities

- Doubting good moments, thinking they won't last

Examples You May Recognize

- Talking yourself out of new opportunities with "It probably won't work"

- Dismissing someone's joy with "That won't last"

- Believing someone's kindness has strings attached

- Overthinking minor flaws while ignoring real progress

- Feeling nervous when life feels "too good"

Why It Needs to Go

Negativity might feel like a shield — but it becomes a cage. It keeps you from vulnerability, yes — but it also blocks growth, joy, and meaningful relationships.

Unchallenged, it can:

- Twist your view of others

- Erode your self-trust

- Keep you locked in cycles of blame or withdrawal

- Turn old wounds into sharp weapons

Letting go of negative thinking isn't about pretending life is perfect — it's about learning to see things clearly, with compassion instead of distortion.

"Your perception of others reveals your relationship with yourself."

How to Overcome It (Step-by-Step)

Step 1: Catch the Projection

Notice when someone triggers a strong reaction in you. Ask yourself:

- What exactly am I accusing them of?

- Is this something I've struggled with myself?

Tracing it back to your own story can be eye-opening.

> *"When you judge another, you do not define them. You define yourself."*
>
> *— Wayne Dyer*

Step 2: Clear Your Inner Dialogue

Often, the way we judge others mirrors how we speak to ourselves.

- Replace internal criticism with self-compassion

- The kinder your self-talk becomes, the more gently you'll view others

- Ask: *"Am I seeing them clearly, or through the lens of my pain?"*

Step 3: Train your Thoughts

When a negative thought pops up, pause and refrain from it.
Examples:

- "They think they're better than me." → *"Maybe they're just confident — and that's okay."*

- "This always goes wrong." → *"I've handled setbacks before. I'll find a way."*

"Change your thoughts and you change your world."

– *Norman Vincent Peale*

Step 4: Celebrate Others Without Comparison

If someone's success makes you feels smaller, shift your mindset from scarcity to abundance.

- Remind yourself: "Their success does not take away from mine."

- Celebrate others out loud — even when it's hard.

- Train your mind to believe: "There's space for all of us to grow."

Step 5: Forgive the Shadow Within

Much of what we project stems from things that we haven't forgiven in ourselves.

- Acknowledge your flaws without judgement

- Speak kindly to your younger; more reactive self

- Remind yourself: *"Healing begins when I stop blaming others for what I haven't faced within*

Try This Today

Think of a recent judgmental or negative thought you had about someone.
Now ask yourself:

- What's really going on beneath this reaction?

- Is this about them — or is it something I've yet to make peace with in myself?

Rewrite the thought with more compassion.

Read it. Let it soften you.

Reflection Prompts

- What kinds of people or situations tend to trigger my negativity?

- What traits in others do I judge— and do they reflect my own insecurities?

- How does this mindset affect my relationships and opportunities?

- Who would I be without the habit of projection or harsh judgment?

- What does it mean to look at the world — and myself — with clarity?

Final Thought to Remember

What you see in others reflects what's unresolved in you. Heal the lens — and the world starts to change.

Chapter 11: Letting Go of Greed — From Craving to Contentment

"Earth provides enough to satisfy every man's needs, but not every man's greed." –Mahatma Gandhi

Understanding the Trait

Greed is often misunderstood. It doesn't always look like wealth-hoarding or ruthless ambition. Sometimes, it appears as a quiet, insatiable hunger — a need for more, no matter how much we already have.

Greed is not the same as ambition.
Ambition is about growth and purpose.
Greed is about possession and control.

Where ambition builds, greed consumes.
Greed whispers, *"It's not enough."*
No matter what you achieve, earn, or attain — it still says, *"More."*

> *"Greed is a fat demon with a small mouth and whatever you feed it is never enough."*
>
> *– Janwillem van de Wetering*

It tricks us into chasing one thing after another, believing happiness is just one more achievement, one more possession, or one more win away — while quietly blinding us to the contentment already within reach.

What It Looks Like in Real Life

- Never feeling truly satisfied, no matter what you gain

- Constantly comparing what you have to what others have

- Making decisions driven by "how much" instead of "is this enough?"

- Sacrificing peace of mind or ethical values for success or gain

- Feeling envious when someone else gets something first — or in greater quantity

- Hoarding time, money, attention, or praise out of fear of losing your advantage

  "Too many people spend money they haven't earned, to buy things they don't want, to impress people they don't like."

  — Will Rogers

Examples You May Recognize

- Always feeling like no matter what you achieve, it's not enough

- Wanting more success or possessions primarily to impress others

- Feeling restless, envious, or dissatisfied when others gain something you don't have

- Prioritizing status or material gains over relationships, peace, or integrity

- Believing happiness is just one more purchase or achievement away

Why It Needs to Go

Greed leads to restlessness, dissatisfaction, and disconnection.

It drives you to:

- Chase without stopping

- Compare without appreciating

- Accumulate without feeling fulfilled

- Compete instead of connect

Worse, it can push you to compromise on your own values — cutting corners, ignoring your conscience, or stepping on others just to get ahead.

"A man is rich in proportion to the number of things which he can afford to let alone."

— Henry David Thoreau

When greed controls you, you're never truly present. You're always living in the "next," the "more," the "not yet."

Letting go of greed means stepping into sufficiency. It's realizing that peace isn't found in having everything — it's found in needing less.

"Contentment is natural wealth. Greed is artificial poverty."

— Socrates

How to Overcome It (Step-by-Step)

Step 1: Define the Difference — Ambition vs. Greed

Ask yourself:

- *"Is this goal aligned with purpose — or driven by fear of lack?"*

- *"Am I building something meaningful — or simply accumulating?"*

Ambition has direction. Greed just has speed.

Step 2: Identify Your "More" Triggers

Where does your mind say, *"Not enough"* most often?

- In money?

- In love or attention?

- In success or recognition?

Naming your triggers helps you understand where your desire is rooted — and whether it's coming from fear or fulfillment.

Step 3: Practice Enoughness

Each day, take a moment to acknowledge:

- What you already have

- What you've already accomplished

- Who is already by your side

Say to yourself:

"This is enough. I am enough."

Gratitude is the antidote to greed.

Step 4: Set Boundaries with Your Desires

You can want more — without needing more.
You can plan — without obsessing.
You can pursue growth — without being consumed by it.

Let desires serve your growth — not govern your peace.

Step 5: Reconnect with Ethical Values

Ask:

- *"Would I still pursue this if I had to sacrifice my values?"*

- *"Does this goal reflect who I truly want to be?"*

Success that comes at the cost of your principles is not success — it's a loss in disguise.

> *"Don't gain the world and lose your soul. Wisdom is better than silver or gold."*
>
> *– Bob Marley*

Try This Today

Write down an area where you often feel it's "never enough."

Now ask yourself the below questions:

- Why do I really want more of this?

- What fear or belief is underneath that desire?

- What would enough look like — and feel like — in this area?

Then, make one conscious choice today to **appreciate** rather than accumulate.

Reflection Prompts

- In what areas of my life do I struggle with "more, more, more"?

- Do I often mistake greed for ambition?

- When was the last time I felt truly content — and what made that possible?

- Have I ever compromised my values for gain?

- What would it mean to live from a place of sufficiency?

Final Thought to Remember

Greed says, "You'll be happy when you have more." Contentment says, "You have enough to be happy now." Choose the voice that sets you free.

Chapter 12: Letting Go of Envy and Comparison — From Lack to Self-Worth

"Comparison is the thief of joy." – Theodore Roosevelt

Understanding the Trait

Envy and comparison are often silent, shameful emotions — hard to admit, but easy to fall into.

They whisper:

- *"Why do they get to have that life?"*

- *"I've worked harder, but they're ahead."*

- *"Everyone's moving forward... except me."*

Envy is the pain of seeing someone else's success and feeling like it takes something away from you. Comparison fuels this pain by measuring your worth, progress, or happiness **against someone else's highlight reel**.

In truth, both envy and comparison stem from **one belief**:
"What I am or have is not enough."

It's important to understand that it's okay to be ambitious. It's okay to want more, to aim higher, to desire growth.

You can pursue big dreams without needing to compare or compete with anyone else.

But it is not okay to feel 'less' because someone else has more.

The only person you should ever compare yourself to is **who you were yesterday.** *"Don't compete with others — compete with your former self."*

What It Looks Like in Real Life

- Scrolling social media and feeling worse about your own life

- Secretly resenting a friend's success, relationship, or appearance

- Minimizing your own wins because they don't feel as "impressive"

- Feeling defeated because someone reached a milestone before you did

- Competing silently — even with people you care about

> *"Envy is the art of counting someone else's blessings instead of your own."*
>
> *– Harold Coffin*

Envy vs. Comparison: What's the Difference?

Trait	Envy	Comparison
Nature	Emotional reaction to perceived inequality	Observation and measurement
Root Thought	"They have what I want — and I feel bad about it."	"Am I doing as well as they are?"
Emotion	Bitterness, sadness, resentment	Insecurity, pressure
Behavior	Passive withdrawal or quiet sabotage	Overanalyzing self-worth
Underlying Belief	"If they win, I lose."	"I'm not enough unless I measure up."

Examples You May Recognize

- You're happy for your friend's engagement — but feel a sting because you're still single.

- A coworker gets praised at work, and instead of celebrating, you start questioning your own competence.

- You stop sharing your creative work because someone else is doing it "better."

- You feel distant from a friend who's thriving — not because they did anything wrong, but because being around them reminds you of your own pain.

"Another person's beauty, success, or light does not dim yours."

Why It Needs to Go

Envy and comparison are deeply self-defeating. They damage relationships, block gratitude, and distort your self-worth. Over time, they:

- Replace **inspiration** with **insecurity**

- Turn **friendship into silent competition**

- Create a **scarcity mindset** — as if there's not enough happiness or success to go around

- Undermine your ability to feel content, present, or proud of your own journey

"You can't compare your chapter 3 to someone else's chapter 30."

If envy and comparison are left unchecked, they often ferment into resentment — not just toward others, but toward life itself. What begins as insecurity can quietly grow into bitterness.

How to Overcome It (Step-by-Step)

Step 1: Catch the Thought Without Shame

When envy or comparison arises, pause and name it:

- *"This is envy."*

- *"I'm comparing myself again."*

You can't heal what you're ashamed to admit.

Step 2: Get Curious, Not Critical

Ask yourself:

- What is this feeling pointing to?

- What desire or insecurity is it highlighting in me?

Maybe it's a longing for love, success, peace, or recognition. Envy reveals the gap between what you want and what you believe you deserve.

Step 3: Return to Your Lane

Remind yourself:

- "Their journey is not mine."

- "What's meant for me won't miss me."

Comparison distracts. Real joy lives in focus.

Step 4: Practice Genuine Celebration

Every time you feel envy, respond with a counteraction:

- Compliment the person sincerely

- Say something uplifting (even silently)

- Remember: *"If it's possible for them, it's possible for me too."*

"When you celebrate others, you train your brain to believe in abundance."

Step 5: Detach From Obsession and Attachment

Envy thrives when you overly attach your selfworth to things — beauty, wealth, lifestyle, status.

People who are obsessed with materialism are more likely to feel envy.
But those who are grounded in values — like peace, compassion, creativity, service — rarely feel threatened by others' success.

"When you no longer chase what others value, you begin to discover what truly fulfills you."

Step 6: Cultivate a Gratitude Habit

Gratitude neutralizes comparison. Start each day by naming:

- 3 things you're proud of

- 3 things you're grateful for

- 1 thing you've overcome

This shifts your thinking from *"not enough"* to *"more than I realized."*

Try This Today

Write a letter to yourself from the perspective of someone who loves and admires you.

Include:

- What makes you unique

- Why your journey is valid and important

- What others might envy in you that you've taken for granted

Let this remind you that you already have more than enough.

Reflection Prompts

- Who do I often compare myself to — and what do I believe they have that I don't?

- What role does materialism or status play in how I judge my worth?

- How does comparison affect my mood, energy, or self-image?

- What personal gifts have I been downplaying because they don't "measure up"?

- What would my life look like if I only measured myself against who I was yesterday?

Final Thought to Remember

You're not behind. You're not less. You're not late. You are on your own unique path — and it's just as worthy. Let go of the race and come back to your own pace.

Chapter 13: Letting Go of Resentment and Grudges — From Past Wounds to Inner Peace

Resentment is like drinking poison and then hoping it will kill your enemies." – Nelson Mandela

Understanding the Trait

Resentment is the quiet, heavy emotion we carry when we've been hurt — and never truly healed. It's the weight of past disappointments, betrayals, injustices, or words that cut too deeply. A grudge is its companion — the mental replay of pain that refuses to release the person who caused it.

At its core, **resentment is re-lived pain**. It replays the moment someone:

- Let you down

- Took advantage of your trust

- Disrespected or misunderstood you

- Chose someone else over you

- Abandoned you without explanation

And instead of healing, we **store the memory like a weapon** — to remind ourselves never to trust again.

But resentment doesn't always stem from obvious harm. Sometimes it begins with comparison — the quiet pain of watching someone else receive what we longed for. Left unaddressed, envy can evolve into bitterness, especially when it feels unfair.

> *"Grudges are burdens too heavy for the heart to bear."*
>
> *— Unknown*

What it Looks Like in Real Life

- Avoiding someone while still thinking about them constantly

- Feeling bitter when their name comes up or they succeed

- Replaying arguments or wrongs over and over in your mind

- Saying, *"I've moved on,"* but feeling emotional when reminded

- Holding imaginary conversations in your head — trying to win, explain, or hurt back

Examples You May Recognize:

- **A friend who betrayed your trust** — You no longer speak, but every time you see their photo or hear their name, something stirs. You tell yourself it's in the past, but the wound still feels fresh.

- **A parent who failed to protect or support you** — You've grown, but the childhood pain hasn't left. You carry silent resentment for what was never given.

- **A partner who cheated or left without closure** — Years may pass, but in your heart, the story still loops. There's no peace — just emotional residue.

- **A colleague who took credit for your work** — You say nothing, but feel wronged, bitter, and undervalued. The anger remains long after the event is over.

"Forgiveness doesn't excuse their behavior. It prevents their behavior from destroying your heart."

— Hemant Smarty

Why It Needs to Go

Resentment is heavy. It chains you to the person or moment that hurt you. The longer you carry it, the more it becomes part of your identity.

Here's what it does to you:

- **Drains your energy** with emotional replays

- **Pollutes your present** with past emotions

- **Limits your ability to trust, love, or feel joy**

- **Turns your pain into your personality**

- **Gives emotional power to the very people who hurt you**

And the longer it goes unspoken, the more resentment can grow — sometimes without you even realizing where it started.

What makes it harder is that the person who hurt you has likely moved on — while you're the one still bleeding.

> *"To forgive is to set a prisoner free,*
> *and discover the prisoner was you."*
>
> – *Lewis B. Smedes*

How to Overcome It (Step-by-Step)

Step 1: Acknowledge the Pain Honestly

You can't let go of something you won't admit is there.

- Write down exactly what happened and how it made you feel

- Don't minimize it — let yourself say: *"That hurt me."*

- Validate your pain before you release it

"Healing begins with honesty."

Step 2: Recognize What You're Still Carrying

What part of the experience still lingers?

- Is it the lack of closure?

- The unfairness?

- The feeling of being replaced, misunderstood, or disrespected?

Name the emotional weight. This gives you clarity on what needs release.

Step 3: Separate the Pain from the Person

This is a turning point.

- Understand that people often act from *their* pain, not yours

- Their behavior doesn't define your worth

- You don't need to reconcile or forget — only to stop bleeding from their actions

"Don't carry the burden of someone else's brokenness."

Step 4: Choose Peace Over Proof

You may never get an apology.
You may never "win" or be understood.
And that's okay.

The goal isn't justice — it's freedom.

- Let go of needing them to "get it"

- Choose inner closure, even if they never offer outer repair

"Peace is not needing closure from those who never gave you peace in the first place."

Step 5: Forgive — Not for Them, But for You

Forgiveness is not approval. It's **emotional release.**

- Forgive to unburden your nervous system

- Forgive to reclaim your present

- Forgive to heal, not to excuse

"Forgiveness isn't forgetting. It's remembering without bitterness."

Step 6: Replace Bitterness With Boundaries

You don't need to allow the same people back in.
You just need to **stop letting them live rent free in your heart.**

- Create distance without drama

- Rebuild your self-trust through healthy boundaries

- Be proud of the peace you've chosen

Try This Today

Write a letter — not to send, but to release.

- Pour out every emotion, hurt, and memory

- Then write: *"I choose to release this so I can heal."*

Tear it up & let it go of it physically as a symbol of releasing it emotionally.

Reflection Prompts

- Who am I still holding emotional weight toward — and why?

- What do I need to say (or hear) to feel closure?

- What has this resentment cost me in energy, joy, or peace?

- Am I willing to forgive, even if I never get an apology?

- What does life feel like without this emotional burden?

- Could some of my resentment be rooted in comparison or envy that I never acknowledged?

Final Thought to Remember

You don't need to win the past. You just need to stop losing yourself to it.

Chapter 14: Letting Go of Expectations — From Disappointment to Emotional Freedom

"Peace begins when expectation ends." – Sri Chinmoy

Understanding the Trait

In the previous chapter, we explored how holding onto past hurts can trap us in cycles of resentment and emotional pain. But there's something that often plants the seed of that resentment long before it even takes root — **expectation**.

Expectations are the silent demands we place on others, situations, and even life itself.

They often go unspoken, but not unfelt.

You expect:

- People to treat you the way you treat them

- Others to understand you without you explaining

- Loved ones to support you in a specific way

- Plans to go exactly how you envisioned

- Life to reward you just because you tried

But when reality doesn't meet those expectations — what follows is almost always **disappointment, frustration, hurt, or anger**.

> *"Unrealistic expectations are premeditated resentments."*
>
> *– Anne Lamott*

This doesn't mean you shouldn't have **standards**, **needs**, or **boundaries** — it means learning the difference between what you can ask for, and what you have no control over.

What It Looks Like in Real Life

- Feeling upset when someone doesn't respond the way you hoped

- Becoming irritated when your efforts aren't noticed or reciprocated

- Getting disappointed when plans don't unfold "as they should"

- Assuming others "should know" what you need without asking

- Carrying silent frustration when people don't act according to your internal script

"Expectation turns relationships into silent negotiations. Disappointment is what's left when no one agreed to the terms."

Examples You May Recognize

- Expecting others to behave exactly how you would — and feeling hurt when they don't

- Feeling upset when plans don't unfold the way you imagined

- Believing your success must follow a perfect timeline or you've failed

- Expecting constant validation, appreciation, or fairness from the world

- Feeling frustrated when reality doesn't match your mental picture

Why It Needs to Go

Expectations, when left unchecked, rob you of peace.
They create invisible emotional contracts with people who didn't sign them.
And they chain your happiness to how well others fulfill your imagined scenarios.

Holding on to rigid expectations:

- Breeds resentment when unmet

- Creates distance in relationships

- Keeps you emotionally dependent

- Fosters blame instead of understanding

- Prevents you from fully accepting the present moment

"The more you expect, the more you suffer. But the less you expect, the more you're free to enjoy what actually is."

Letting go of expectations doesn't mean lowering your worth — it means choosing peace over pressure.

How to Overcome It (Step-by-Step)

Step 1: Identify the Silent Agreements

Ask yourself:

- "What unspoken contract am I holding this person to?"

- "Did I clearly express my needs, or did I assume?"

- "Am I expecting someone to do something I haven't done myself?"

Awareness breaks the pattern.

Step 2: Differentiate Needs from Control

A need sounds like: "I value honesty in relationships."
An expectation sounds like: "You should always respond the way I want."

Ask:

"Is this something I truly need — or something I'm trying to control?"

Honor your needs. Loosen your grip on control.

Step 3: Replace Assumptions with Communication

Expectations often live in silence.
Instead, speak.

Say:

- "It would mean a lot to me if..."

- "I feel disappointed when..."

- "Can we talk about what we both hope for?"

Clarity is more loving than assumption.

Step 4: Allow Life to Unfold Without a Script

Plans are useful. Scripts are restrictive.
Let go of the idea that things *must* happen a certain way.

"Even if things don't go as I imagined, I trust they're unfolding in the way that's best for me."

Open hands make room for grace.

Step 5: Return to the Present Moment

Expectation pulls you into imaginary futures.
Come back to what's real — here and now.

Breathe. Notice. Accept. Respond.

"Peace is not having things your way — it's finding calm in whatever way things come."

Try This Today

Think of a recent moment where you felt disappointed or let down. Now ask yourself:

- What expectation was hiding behind that feeling?

- Did I express it clearly — or only carry it silently?

- What can I let go of in this moment to feel free again?

Reflection Prompts

- What areas of my life are most shaped by expectation?

- Which expectations have caused me the most frustration or disappointment?

- Do I tend to assume others know what I want or need?

- How would I feel if I focused on expressing, not expecting?

- What would emotional freedom look like for me?

Final Thought to Remember

Expectations tie your peace to someone else's actions. Letting go unties the knot — and brings you back to yourself.

Chapter 15: Letting Go of Victim Identity — From Self-Pity to Personal Strength

"You either walk inside your story and own it, or you stand outside your story and hustle for your worthiness." — Brené Brown

Understanding the Trait

Victim identity is a mindset built on pain, shaped by self-pity, and fed by the belief that everything happening *to* you is unfair. It keeps you locked in cycles of helplessness, blame, and emotional exhaustion.

At the heart of this identity is **self-pity** — the quiet voice that says:

- *"Why does this always happen to me?"*

- *"No one understands how difficult my life is."*

- *"I try so hard, but nothing ever works out for me."*

Self-pity is the seed. Victim mentality is the root system it grows into.

What It Looks Like in Real Life

- Constantly feeling wronged, overlooked, or unlucky

111

- Refusing help or advice, yet complaining about problems

- Emotionally withdrawing while hoping others will "see" your pain

- Blaming people, fate, or the past for current stagnation

- Avoiding responsibility by saying, "There's nothing I can do about it"

Examples You May Recognize

- A person who was betrayed in a past relationship, and now says:
"All people are untrustworthy. I'm always the one who gets hurt."

- Someone who constantly says *"I'm just unlucky"*, instead of examining how their patterns or mindset may be contributing to repeated disappointments.

- A person who doesn't try for new opportunities because they've already told themselves: *"People like me never make it."*

Self-Pity vs. Victim Mentality What's the Difference?

Trait	Self-Pity	Victim Mentality
Focus	Emotion (pain)	Identity (pattern)
Thoughts	"This hurts so much."	"The world is unfair to me."
Behavior	Withdrawal, tears, rumination	Blame, avoidance, passive aggression
Need	Comfort, validation	Control without responsibility
Root Emotion	Sadness	Helplessness & resentment
Hidden Belief	"I'm alone in this."	"I can't change anything."

"Victimhood feels like protection, but it's actually imprisonment."

"Victimhood feels like protection but it's actually imprisonment."

Why It Needs to Go

Carrying a victim identity may offer emotional comfort in the short term — it gives a story, a justification, a reason to stay still. But long term, it becomes a cage. It disempowers your ability to grow, take action, and transform.

Here's what it costs:

- Your power to act

- Your peace of mind

- Your connection with others

- Your ability to heal and move forward

"You can't heal while holding on to a story that says you're worthless."

This mindset also repels genuine support — because people grow weary of comforting someone who is unwilling to rise. And most importantly, you start to believe your own limitations.

How to Overcome It (Step-by-Step)

Step 1: Name the Story You've Been Repeating

Every victim identity has a story behind it.

- "People always leave me."

- "I'm not good enough."

- "Others succeed because they had it easier."

Write your story down honestly. Seeing it clearly is the first step to breaking free.

Step 2: Validate the Pain, But Don't Live There

You are allowed to feel hurt, betrayed, or disappointed. But you are not meant to stay in that emotional state forever.

Say to yourself:
"This happened to me, and it hurt... but it doesn't have to define me."

"You can honor your pain without turning it into your personality."

Step 3: Take Ownership of What You Can Control

There is always something within your reach:

- Your mindset

- Your reaction

- Your next decision

- Your words and actions

Start small. Start now. Ownership = freedom.

Step 4: Watch Your Words

Stop reinforcing helplessness in your language.

Replace:

- "I can't..." → "I choose to..."

- "This always happens to me..." → "This happened, now how can I respond differently?"

Words shape identity — speak with strength.

Step 5: Reconnect with Your Strength

Make a list of times you were resilient.
Remind yourself of the storms you've survived.
Say to yourself:
"I may have been broken, but I was never defeated."

Your past is proof that you are stronger than your story.

Step 6: Rewrite the Narrative

If your old story was *"Life is unfair to me,"*
Try:
" I have faced many challenges in my life — but I'm still standing, and I choose to rise."

Try This Today

Write a letter to your past self from your present strength.

Start with:
"I know you've been through a lot, but you are not worthless. You are capable. You are healing and I won't let this story define us anymore."

Keep it. Remind yourself when the victim voice creeps back in.

Reflection Prompts

- What emotional story have I been repeating to myself — and is it still serving me?

- In what ways do I avoid responsibility by blaming others, fate, or the past?

- What does my victim voice sound like — and how can I challenge it with strength?

- How would my life look if I showed up as the main character, not a background one?

- What does personal strength mean to me — and how can I embody that today?

Final Thought to Remember

You are not what happened to you — you are who you choose to become. The moment you stop

117

identifying as a victim, you begin rising as a victor.

Chapter 16: Letting Go of the Need for Control — From Force to Flow

"You must learn to let go. Release the stress. You were never in control anyway." – *Steve Maraboli*

Understanding the Trait

The need for control is not always loud. Sometimes it looks like overplanning, micromanaging, perfectionism, or endless anxiety. Other times, it hides behind helpfulness or high standards. But beneath the surface, it's almost always rooted in one thing: **fear**.

"If I control everything, I can protect myself."
"If I stay prepared, nothing bad will happen."

It's not about wanting power — it's about trying to feel safe. Often, those who crave control have experienced some form of unpredictability, chaos, or emotional instability in the past. And now, their nervous system confuses *control* with *security*.

The tighter we hold on, the more we feel responsible for **everything** — not just our own choices, but other people's reactions, outcomes, timelines, and emotions. It becomes exhausting, overwhelming, and unsustainable.

And perhaps worst of all, it shuts out one of life's greatest teachers: **flow**.

"Control is the illusion. Trust is the truth."

What It Looks Like in Real Life

- Feeling tense or panicked when plans change

- Micromanaging tasks or people to ensure a "perfect" outcome

- Struggling to delegate or let others take the lead

- Rehearsing conversations, outcomes, or risks obsessively

- Trying to plan every detail of life to avoid disappointment

- Feeling deeply uncomfortable with uncertainty or spontaneity

Examples You May Recognize

- A parent who schedules every second of their child's life, not out of discipline, but out of fear of failure

- A team leader who struggles to trust others' decisions, believing no one else will "do it right"

- A friend who obsesses over social gatherings — not for fun, but to avoid the discomfort of chaos or awkwardness

- Someone who won't take action unless they're certain of the outcome, staying stuck in inaction disguised as control

"Needing to control everything is often a trauma response dressed up as responsibility."

Why It Needs to Go

Control is heavy. It makes you tense, anxious, and reactive. It builds walls between you and others. It tells you that the only way to feel safe is to manage everything and everyone.

Here's what it costs:

- **Your peace of mind**

- **Your ability to rest**

- **Your openness to surprise, creativity, or spontaneity**

- **Your relationships** — because people don't want to be managed, they want to be trusted

- **Your flexibility** — when life inevitably changes, you suffer more than you need to

"You cannot heal if you are always trying to control how healing happens."

How to Overcome It (Step-by-Step)

Step 1: Acknowledge What You're Really Afraid Of

The desire to control is often masking a fear:

- Fear of failure

- Fear of disappointment

- Fear of not being enough

- Fear of being hurt again

Ask yourself: *"What am I trying to protect myself from?"*

Naming the fear weakens its grip.

Step 2: Separate Control From Competence

Being responsible is good.
Being thoughtful is good.
But control crosses the line when it:

- Suffocates creativity

- Disrespects others' space

- Replaces intuition with rigid logic

- Disconnects you from the moment

Let go of the lie that says *"If I'm not in control, I'm failing."*

Step 3: Shift From Force to Flow

Control says: "Push harder."
Flow says: "Move with it."

Start small:

- Let someone else lead a task

- Allow a plan to be flexible

- Accept that not everything will go your way — and that's okay

"You're allowed to take your hands off the wheel sometimes — life won't crash."

Step 4: Learn the Language of Trust

Practice trusting:

- Yourself: "I can handle whatever happens."

- Others: "They have their own journey."

- Life: "Even if it's uncertain, I can still grow through it."

Control says: *"I need guarantees."*
Trust says: *"I need peace more than certainty."*

Step 5: Breathe When Control Creeps In

When control urges rise:

- Pause

- Breathe deeply

- Ask: *"Am I reacting from fear right now?"*

- Remind yourself: *"I can release what's not mine to carry."*

Even 60 seconds of awareness can shift your response.

Try This Today

Pick one thing you usually control — a routine, a task, a plan — and consciously **let it be imperfect**. Let someone else take over. Allow life to unfold.

Then reflect: *"Did things fall apart... or did I simply survive the discomfort of not being in charge?"*

Reflection Prompts

- What do I try to control — and why?

- What am I scared off will happen if I let go?

- How does my need for control affect the people around me?

- Where in my life could I create more flow, trust, or flexibility?

- What would it feel like to rest without feeling guilty?

Final Thought to Remember

Letting go of control doesn't mean giving up — it means giving space. Space for life to surprise you, for others to grow, and for yourself to breathe.

Chapter 17: Letting Go of Overthinking — From Chaos to Clarity

"Rule your mind or it will rule you." –Buddha

Understanding the Trait

Overthinking is a silent thief. It doesn't steal your time all at once — it chips away at your energy, clarity, and peace of mind, one thought loop at a time.

It convinces you that thinking more will protect you. That if you just analyze it enough, you'll avoid mistakes, pain, or regret. But in truth, overthinking is not a shield — it's a cage.

Instead of helping you move forward, it traps you in a cycle of doubt, worry, and mental exhaustion.

At its root, overthinking often comes from:

- Fear of the unknown

- Fear of making the wrong decision

- Low self-trust

- The illusion that "more thinking" means more control

You may believe you're preparing. But what you're really doing is **postponing peace**.

"Overthinking is the art of creating problems that weren't even there."

It's okay to reflect. It's okay to plan. But when thinking becomes looping — and clarity never comes — you've left the realm of helpful thought and entered mental chaos.

What It Looks Like in Real Life

- Replaying conversations and wishing you'd said something different

- Trying to plan for every possible outcome before making a move

- Mentally rehearsing or defending yourself before anything has happened

- Questioning if people are upset with you without any clear reason

- Staying stuck in decisions, afraid to choose wrong

- Worrying excessively about the future or regretting the past

- Feeling emotionally tense, but unable to explain why

Examples You May Recognize

- A person who writes and rewrites a message multiple times, never pressing send

- Someone who mentally prepares for every possible "what if" before attending a simple event

- A friend who can't sleep because they're replaying something they said a week ago

- A person who wants to start something new — a project, a relationship, a move — but remains frozen in "what ifs" and "what might go wrong"

"Thinking too much doesn't create clarity — it creates confusion disguised as caution."

Types of Overthinking and Their Emotional Impact

Type of Overthinking	How It Feels	What It Leads To
Replaying the past	Regret, guilt, or shame	Dwelling, emotional fatigue
Fear of future outcomes	Anxiety, dread, nervousness	Inaction, avoidance, poor sleep
Overanalyzing people's opinions	Self-doubt, people-pleasing	Social anxiety, hiding your true self
Perfection-based decision paralysis	Pressure, confusion	Missed opportunities, procrastination
Mental rehearsing & self-defense	Tension, insecurity	Emotional burnout, fear of vulnerability

Why It Needs to Go

Overthinking wears the mask of wisdom — but it's really fear in disguise.

It convinces you that you're being responsible, cautious, or prepared. But deep down, it's often your mind trying to **avoid discomfort** — not embrace growth.

Here's what it slowly steals:

- Your presence and peace

- Your confidence in decision making

- Your ability to act and move forward

- Your mental and emotional energy

- Your connection with reality

"The mind was meant to think — but not nonstop. Even the best engines need rest."

When your thoughts become endless loops, you're not solving anything — you're **reliving imaginary versions of the problem**, without resolution.

And the longer you stay in that mental loop, the further you drift from clarity.

How to Overcome It (Step-by-Step)

Step 1: Recognize the Loop Without Judgment

Overthinking is not a personal failure — it's a habit.
The first step is catching it.

Say gently:
"I'm looping again."
"This isn't productive thought — this is worry disguised as control."

Awareness creates pause.

Step 2: Ask "Is This Helping or Hurting?"

When a thought repeats more than twice, stop and ask:

- Is this helping me take action?

- Is it giving me clarity?

- Or is it draining and confusing me?

If it's not helpful, gently redirect.

Step 3: Use "Mental Boundaries"

Just like physical boundaries protect your space, mental boundaries protect your peace.

- Set a **time limit** for decision making (e.g., "I'll reflect for 20 minutes, then choose.")

- Delay looping by writing it down and returning later

- Create a mental "stop sign" when thoughts spiral unnecessarily

"Your mind is a tool, not your master."

Step 4: Anchor Yourself in the Present

Overthinking often pulls you into the past or future.

Use your senses to return to now:

- Feel your feet on the floor

- Take deep, intentional breaths

- Ask: *"What's actually happening right now?"*

Peace lives in the present — not in the imagined.

Step 5: Trust Your Inner Wisdom

You don't need to overthink when you trust yourself.

Remind yourself:

- "Not knowing everything doesn't mean I'm failing."

- "Good decisions come from clarity — not panic."

The more you trust your intuition, the less you'll need to over-plan or overcontrol.

Try This Today

Pick one decision or situation you've been overthinking.

Now:

- Set a timer for 15 minutes

- Write down your thoughts once

- At the end of the timer, either make a decision or let it go

Tell yourself: "I choose clarity, not chaos."

Reflection Prompts

- What do I tend to overthink — and what am I afraid of underneath it?

- How does overthinking affect my sleep, energy, or confidence?

- What would it feel like to trust my ability to figure things out as I go?

- Where in my life do I confuse thinking with solving?

- How can I remind myself that peace matters more than perfection?

Final Thought to Remember

You don't need to figure everything out right now. Let go of the endless loops, and let clarity come through calm. Some answers only appear when the mind is still.

Chapter 18: Letting Go of Anger — From Reaction to Response

"Speak when you are angry, and you will make the best speech you will ever regret." – Ambrose Bierce

Understanding the Trait

Anger is one of the most powerful emotions — and also one of the most misunderstood.

It often arises in response to:

- Feeling disrespected, hurt, or betrayed

- Experiencing injustice or unfair treatment

- Suppressed pain or grief

- Unmet needs or boundaries being crossed

- A sense of helplessness or lack of control

At its core, anger is a signal — a fiery flare telling you that **something matters deeply** to you. But when left unprocessed, it becomes **destructive** rather than instructive.

"Anger is not the enemy. It's what we do with it that defines the damage."

Unexpressed anger may harden into bitterness or resentment. Unleashed in harmful ways, it can lead to **guilt, regret, or shame**, especially when it goes against your values. Either way, when anger controls you, it blocks clarity, peace, and connection.

What It Looks Like in Real Life

- Yelling, snapping, or becoming passive-aggressive during minor frustrations

- Holding grudges long after a conflict ends

- Getting irritated easily, then feeling guilty or distant afterward

- Silently seething instead of communicating openly

- Using sarcasm or withdrawal as a shield

- Feeling triggered by unresolved pain from the past

Examples You May Recognize

- Someone who lashes out in traffic but is really carrying stress from work or home

- A parent who explodes at their child — not out of malice, but because they're emotionally exhausted

- A friend who gives the silent treatment instead of expressing what hurt them

- A person who replays a betrayal years later, still carrying the emotional weight of it

Why It Needs to Go

Anger, when unchecked, becomes a prison. It may feel powerful in the moment, but it leaves you feeling:

- Emotionally drained

- Reactive instead of reflective

- Disconnected from people you care about

- Clouded in judgment

- Trapped in cycles of conflict or guilt

"You cannot heal while holding on to rage. Anger may be the fire, but it is not the freedom."

Letting go of anger doesn't mean you tolerate injustice or suppress your voice. It means you choose **clarity over chaos**, **response over reaction**, and **self-control over self-destruction**.

How to Overcome It (Step-by-Step)

Step 1: Acknowledge the Real Emotion Underneath

Anger is often a surface emotion — a mask for something deeper.

Beneath anger, you may find:

- Hurt

- Fear

- Disappointment

- Grief

- Feeling unseen or misunderstood

- Frustration, envy, or hatred that hasn't been dealt with

Ask yourself: *"What am I really feeling beneath the fire?"*

Naming the true emotion doesn't make you weaker — it gives that emotion a healthy, honest way to be seen.

Step 2: Create Space Between Trigger and Reaction

When you feel anger rising:

- Pause

- Breathe

- Step away if needed

- Remind yourself: *"I'm allowed to feel this — but I can choose how to express it."*

The space between trigger and response is where self-mastery lives.

> *"The strong is not the one who overcomes the people by his strength, but the strong is the one who controls himself while in anger."*
>
> *— Prophet Muhammad (Peace be upon Him)- Prophet of Islam*

Step 3: Express, Don't Explode or Suppress

You don't have to silence your anger — but you don't have to let it consume you either.

Healthy expression may look like:

- Writing your thoughts down

- Talking to someone you trust

- Saying how you feel in a calm, assertive way

Examples of assertive language:

- "I feel disrespected when this happens."

- "I need a moment to calm down before we continue."

- "I'm upset, but I want to talk this through respectfully."

Feeling angry is normal — what matters is choosing to control it, so it doesn't control you or harm those around you.

Step 4: Let Go for the Sake of Your Own Peace

You may never get the apology. You may never hear the words you needed to hear.

But you can choose peace anyway.

"I no longer carry this anger — I choose peace over pain."

Step 5: Set Boundaries Before Anger Builds

Sometimes anger erupts because our boundaries were never voiced.

Learn to speak your needs calmly and early:

- "That's not okay with me."

- "I would appreciate if you would respect my time."

- "This is what I'm comfortable with — and what I'm not."

Boundaries prevent explosions. They protect your energy before resentment forms.

Try This Today

Think of a situation or person that still triggers anger within you.
Now ask:

- *"What emotion is really hiding behind this anger?"*

- *"Is this emotion asking for healing, not conflict?"*

- *"What would releasing this free me to feel instead?"*

Anger blocks the heart. Letting it go makes space for peace.

Reflection Prompts

- What situations make me most reactive — and why?

- What deeper emotions are hiding beneath my anger?

- How has my anger affected my relationships and energy?

- Do I explode, suppress, or express my anger in healthy ways?

- What would strength look like for me in moments of anger?

Final Thought to Remember

True strength isn't shown through rage — it's shown through restraint. Those who control their anger are among the strongest of all, while those who unleash it without control lack strength and self-mastery.

Chapter 19: Letting Go of Dwelling in the Past — From Memory Loops to Presence

"The past is a place of reference, not a place of residence." – Roy T. Bennett

Understanding the Trait

Dwelling in the past doesn't always look the same. Sometimes it's the **painful replay of regrets, trauma, or betrayal**. Other times, it's the **longing for the "good old days"** — when life felt easier, happier, or more fulfilling.

Whether it's pain or nostalgia, the result is the same: **your mind gets stuck somewhere you no longer live**, and your present begins to slip away.

"We don't move forward when our thoughts keep turning backward."

While remembering the past is human and even healthy in moderation, the problem begins when:

- The past becomes your identity

- Your thoughts loop without resolution

- You use the past to justify your present stagnation

- You resist fully engaging with today because yesterday felt better — or worse

Dwelling in the past keeps you emotionally anchored to what *was*, making it nearly impossible to create what *could be*.

What It Looks Like in Real Life

- Replaying old conversations, arguments, or decisions over and over

- Constantly saying, *"If only I had..."* or *"I wish I could go back"*

- Idealizing a former time and resenting the present for not measuring up

- Refusing to forgive others — or yourself — for past actions

- Feeling stuck emotionally, like a part of you never left a certain chapter of life

Examples You May Recognize

- Someone who can't let go of a relationship that ended years ago, holding on to memories as if they're still real

- A parent who keeps comparing the joy of raising young children to the emptiness they now feel

- A person who repeatedly replays a mistake, career loss, or betrayal, hoping it will somehow "make sense"

- Someone who uses a past success to avoid taking new risks — afraid they'll never "get back there" again

"You can't start the next chapter of your life if you keep re-reading the last one."

"Both grief and nostalgia can become cages if you don't let yourself grow beyond them."

Why It Needs to Go

The past is a **teacher** — not a home. When you live in it, even mentally, you begin to **disconnect from your ability to grow, enjoy, and take action in the now**.

Here's what dwelling in the past slowly takes from you:

- Your energy and attention

- Your sense of possibility

- Your relationships (because you're not truly present)

- Your ability to forgive, release, and evolve

- Your capacity for joy, gratitude, and renewal

"If you carry yesterday into today, you lose both."

145

But that doesn't mean you should erase the past. The past is meant to:

- **Teach you** through experience

- **Show you** what you've overcome

- **Remind you** to be grateful for what once was

Just don't let it define you — or distract you from who you're becoming.

How to Overcome It (Step-by-Step)

Step 1: Identify What You're Holding Onto

Ask yourself:

- *"What moment from the past do I keep replaying?"*

- *"Is it rooted in pain, regret... or longing?"*

Naming it helps you step outside of it.

Step 2: Ask What It's Costing You

Reflect honestly:

- What is dwelling on this stopping me from doing today?

- Who am I not becoming because I keep looking backward?

Sometimes we hold onto the past because it's familiar — but growth only happens in forward motion.

Step 3: Honor the Past, Don't Worship It

Feel the emotions. Remember what happened.

But then remind yourself:

"This happened. I learned. I lived. And now I move forward."

You are allowed to appreciate the past without needing to stay in it.

Step 4: Turn Memory Into Meaning

Instead of asking, *"Why did this happen?"*, ask:

- *"What did this teach me?"*

- *"How did this shape my strength, resilience, or values?"*

Let the past be a lesson, not a limitation.

Step 5: Anchor Back Into the Present

Practice bringing your awareness back to *now*:

- Focus on your breath

- Observe your surroundings without judgment

- Say: *"I am here. I am safe. I am free to begin again."*

You can visit the past — but don't live there.

Try This Today

Write a letter to your past self.
Tell them:

- What you've learned

- What you're grateful for

- What you're ready to release

Then write one sentence to your future self that starts with:

"From this day forward, I choose to..."

Reflection Prompts

- What memory or time in my life do I find myself emotionally living in?

- Do I dwell more in past — or in present?

- How has living in the past affected my ability to be present?

- What lessons from the past can I honor without clinging to?

- What would my life feel like if I embraced today fully?

Final Thought to Remember

The past is a place to visit, not to stay. Learn from it, feel gratitude for it, and then gently return to the only place you can truly live — the present.

Chapter 20: Letting Go of Fear of Change — From Resistance to Growth

"Change is hard at first, messy in the middle, and beautiful at the end." — Robin Sharma

Understanding the Trait

Change is one of the most inevitable and essential parts of life — yet also one of the most resisted.

Why?
Because change asks us to:

- Leave the familiar

- Step into the unknown

- Release control

- Trust what's unfolding

Fear of change isn't weakness — it's the mind's attempt to protect us from discomfort, unpredictability, or perceived danger. But while that fear may feel like safety, it quietly becomes a prison that prevents growth, renewal, and transformation.

"We don't fear change itself — we fear losing control, losing comfort, or losing identity."

There's a part of you that longs to evolve — but there may also be a part clinging tightly to what's known, even if it no longer serves you.

And that tug-of-war between growth and resistance creates internal tension.

What It Looks Like in Real Life

- Staying in unfulfilling jobs, relationships, or environments out of fear of the unknown

- Postponing decisions, waiting for the "perfect" time

- Rejecting new opportunities or paths because they feel risky

- Feeling stuck but afraid to make a move

- Clinging to routines or roles because they feel safe, even if they feel empty

"Sometimes, what we call 'stability' is just a fear of outgrowing our current self."

Examples You May Recognize

- Staying in a job, relationship, or situation that makes you unhappy because it's familiar

- Resisting new opportunities because they feel risky or uncomfortable

- Feeling anxious even about positive changes (like success, growth, new beginnings)

- Clinging to old habits or roles even when they've outlived their purpose

- Choosing "the known" over "the possible" even when you feel stuck

Why It Needs to Go

When you fear change, you hold on to your old self — and miss the chance to grow into your true self.

It prevents you from:

- Starting the journey

- Taking new opportunities

- Reinventing your life

- Trusting your own resilience

But when you learn to release that fear, even gradually, you open the door to a life that's richer, freer, and more aligned with who you truly are.

"Change may feel like loss — but it's often the path to something greater."

How to Overcome It (Step-by-Step)

Step 1: Acknowledge the Fear Honestly

Don't deny it.
Ask yourself:

- "What exactly am I afraid of losing?"

- "What discomfort am I trying to avoid?"

Naming the fear is the first step to disarming it.

Step 2: Separate Actual Risk from Imagined Fear

Not all fear is factual. Much of it is a story your mind creates.

Ask yourself:

- "What's the worst that could happen and will I be able to handle it?"

- "What might go right if I embraced this change?"

Most often, you'll find the fear is louder than the actual risk.

Step 3: Reframe Change as Growth, Not Threat

Instead of asking:

- *"What if I fail?"*

Ask yourself:

- *"What might I learn?"*

- *"What new part of me might emerge?"*

Shift your lens from fear to curiosity.

Step 4: Take One Small Step Forward

You don't need to overhaul everything overnight.
Pick one small move:

- Research the new path

- Say yes to one new opportunity

- Let go of one limiting routine

Movement builds momentum — and confidence.

Step 5: Trust That Growth Is Your Natural State

You were never meant to stay the same.
Change isn't an interruption to life — it **is** life.

"A flower doesn't resist blooming because it fears the wind. It opens anyway."

Let this be your season to open.

Try This Today

Write down one change you've been resisting.

Then answer:

- What fear is holding me back?

- What could this change help me grow into?

- What's one small action I can take to begin moving forward — today?

Reflection Prompts

- What am I afraid will happen if I embrace change?

- What might I lose — and what might I gain?

- Where in my life am I holding on too tightly?

- What's one change I once feared that turned out to be a blessing?

- Who might I become if I stop resisting?

Final Thought to Remember

You don't have to feel ready to grow — you just have to be willing. Change isn't here to break you. It's here to awaken you.

A Pause Before the Becoming Begins

You've just walked through twenty powerful chapters — not just reading, but reflecting, unlearning, and releasing. You've loosened the grip of people pleasing, silenced the noise of comparison, laid down the weight of resentment, and taken your first steps away from the fears and patterns that once held you back.

This wasn't easy work.
Letting go never is.
But it is necessary.

What you've done so far is like clearing out a long-carried burden — shedding the layers, loosening the ties, and making space within yourself for something new.
Now, the space is ready.
And what you choose to build next will define not just how you grow, but who you become.

Part 1 was about release.
Part 2 will be about rebuilding.
It's about choosing the traits, the mindset, and the identity that align with your truest self.

Before you continue, pause for a moment.
Breathe.
Honor the effort you've made.
You've let go of the weights. Now, it's time to rise.

PART 2:

WHAT TO BUILD WITHIN

·

Part 2 — What to Build Within

This is where the building begins — quietly, intentionally, from the inside out.

You've done the hard work of letting go — releasing what no longer serves you, loosening the burdens of fear, guilt, self doubt, and painful patterns.

Now, the space within you is clear — and ready.

This next part of your journey is about choosing what to strengthen.
Not just surface habits — but deep-rooted values, principles, and perspectives that support your growth long after the reading ends.

In the chapters ahead, you'll cultivate:
Self-awareness and purpose
Integrity and authenticity
Motivation, confidence, and discipline Emotional resilience and empathy
Gratitude, mindfulness, and true contentment

These are not temporary improvements.
 They are the foundation of who you are becoming.

You're no longer carrying the old weights.
You're now building your inner core — with clarity, intention, and care.

This is the beginning of your becoming.

Chapter 21: Self Awareness & Reflection — The Foundation of Inner Growth

"Knowing yourself is the beginning of all wisdom."–Aristotle

Understanding the Trait

Self-awareness is the ability to observe yourself with clarity—to see your thoughts, behaviors, emotions, and patterns without denial or distortion. It's the inner mirror that allows you to understand not just what you do, but why you do it.

Introspection is the deeper process of pausing and looking inward. It helps you examine your thoughts, understand your emotions, and process your daily experiences through a more conscious lens.

(Introspection, often referred to as reflection, is the deliberate practice of examining your inner world so you can respond to life more intentionally.)

Together, self-awareness and introspection form the foundation of personal growth.
They help you interrupt reactive habits, recognize internal patterns, and course-correct with purpose.

"The first step toward change is awareness. The second step is acceptance."

– Nathaniel Branden

People who lack self-awareness may:

- React impulsively without understanding the root of their emotions

- Repeat harmful patterns in relationships or decisions

- Struggle to take accountability or recognize their impact on others

- Constantly feel disconnected from their actions, goals, or even identity

True self-awareness is not self-criticism. It is clarity without judgment.
It allows you to notice without condemning and to correct without shaming.

"Self-awareness doesn't stop you from making mistakes, it allows you to learn from them."

– Unknown

Introspection turns experiences into insight. It gives you the ability to grow from within instead of merely reacting to life from the outside.

Why It Matters

You can't change what you don't see.
You can't grow from what you never pause to understand.

Self-awareness empowers you to:

- Recognize your emotional triggers and respond with intention

- Align your actions with your values

- Understand your strengths and weaknesses honestly

- Break free from autopilot living

- Strengthen your relationships through clearer communication and boundaries

  "Awareness is the greatest agent for change."

  – Eckhart Tolle

When you develop self-awareness, life becomes less about reacting—and more about choosing. You begin to notice your patterns, catch yourself in the moment, and live more in alignment with who you want to be.

Introspection, meanwhile, offers the gift of perspective. It slows down the noise of life and gives you space to connect with your deeper self—so you don't just live, but live consciously.

How to Cultivate It (Step-by-Step)

Step 1: Observe Without Judgment

Notice your thoughts, reactions, and emotions throughout the day.
Don't rush to label them as good or bad—just observe them.

Say to yourself, "That's interesting," instead of, "That's wrong."

Step 2: Ask Yourself Better Questions

Rather than "What's wrong with me?"
Ask:

- "What triggered me just now?"

- "What am I really feeling beneath this reaction?"

- "What do I need in this moment?

  The quality of your self-awareness is shaped by the quality of your questions.

  —Anthony Robbins

Step 3: Practice Daily Introspection

Spend a few minutes each evening reviewing your day.
Ask:

- *"Where did I feel most aligned with myself today?"*

- *"Where did I feel off or disconnected?"*

- *"What did I learn about myself?"*

This small habit turns daily moments into lifelong wisdom.

Step 4: Listen to Feedback Without Defensiveness

Sometimes others can see blind spots we miss.
Instead of rejecting feedback, reflect on it.
Ask,
"Is there a part of this that's true?"

Use it not as a weapon, but as a mirror.

Step 5: Make Self-Check-Ins a Habit

Pause throughout the day and ask:

- "What am I feeling right now?"

- "Why am I choosing this?"

- "Is this reaction aligned with who I want to be?"

Self-awareness isn't a one-time event— it's a daily practice of returning to yourself.

Try This Today

Set aside five minutes tonight and write down answers to these three prompts:

- One moment today I felt truly myself was...

- One moment I acted out of habit or emotion was...

- Tomorrow, I want to be more aware of...

Start simple. Consistency is more powerful than perfection.

Reflection Prompts

- What patterns do I repeat in my reactions or choices?

- When do I feel most aligned with my true self—and when do I feel furthest from it?

- Do I spend more time judging myself or learning from myself?

- How do I respond when someone points out something I don't see in myself?

- What role does introspection play in my current decision-making?

Final Thought to Remember

The path to growth begins not with perfection, but with self-honesty. Awareness is the first act of transformation.

Chapter 22: Purpose-Driven Mindset — Living with Direction, Not Just Motion

"Efforts and courage are not enough without purpose and direction." – John F. Kennedy

Understanding the Trait

A purpose-driven mindset is about living intentionally — making choices that align with something greater than comfort, approval, or routine. It means having a reason behind your actions, a direction behind your growth, and a "why" behind your goals.

It's not about knowing every detail of your future. It's about having clarity on what truly matters — and letting that shape the way you show up in the world.

> *"He who has a why to live can bear almost any how."*
>
> *– Friedrich Nietzsche*

Purpose and values are closely linked. You cannot live with direction if you don't know what you stand for. A life driven by purpose is, at its core, a life driven by values. Your purpose grows out of your deepest convictions — and

167

when you live by those convictions, you lead yourself with greater confidence, clarity, and consistency.

People without a sense of purpose often:

- Drift from one task to another without meaning

- Feel busy but not fulfilled

- Struggle to commit or persevere through challenges

- Chase goals that aren't truly their own

A life without purpose may be full — but it rarely feels meaningful.

Why It Matters

Living with purpose gives your life weight and direction.
It keeps you grounded during setbacks, focused during distractions, and fulfilled in ways that success alone cannot offer.

When you know your "why," you:

- Make clearer decisions

- Say "no" to what doesn't align

- Bounce back quicker from failure

- Feel more energized and connected to your daily life

"Lack of direction, not lack of time, is the problem. We all have 24-hour days."

– Zig Ziglar

Purpose also simplifies your path.
It doesn't eliminate effort — it just makes the effort feel worth it.

"Success is not the result of endless movement, but of intentional direction."

– Unknown

How to Cultivate It (Step-by-Step)

Step 1: Define What Matters Most to You

Purpose isn't found — it's uncovered. Start by asking yourself:

- *"What kind of impact do I want to have?"*

- *"What problems do I feel inclined to solve?"*

- *"What makes me feel deeply alive or at peace?"*

Purpose often sits where your values and passions meet the needs of others.

Step 2: Clarify Your Core Values

Purpose is rooted in principles. List your top 3–5 values — things like service, growth, truth, compassion, justice, or creativity.

Then ask yourself:

- *"Am I living in alignment with these values?"*

- *"What choices reflect or violate these values?"*

  "When you are clear on your values, decision-making becomes easier."

  –Roy Disney

Step 3: Align Your Goals With Your Why

Make sure your goals serve your deeper purpose — not just your ego or expectations.

Ask:

- *"Why do I want this?"*

- *"Would I still want it if no one noticed?"*

Choose goals that move your life toward meaning — not just metrics.

Step 4: Say No to Distractions That Dilute You

A purposeful life requires focus. Not everything that comes your way is meant for you.

Remind yourself:

- *"Just because I can doesn't mean I should."*

- *"If it doesn't serve my purpose, it doesn't deserve my energy."*

Try This Today

Write down your answer to this question:
"If I could devote my energy to one meaningful cause, contribution, or value — what would it be?"

Then list one small way to live that purpose today — no matter how simple.

Reflection Prompts

- What gives my life meaning beyond achievement?

- When do I feel most aligned with something bigger than myself?

- What do I want to stand for — even if I never get credit for it?

- What distractions tend to pull me away from purpose?

- How would my life change if I lived with more intention?

Final Thought to Remember

Purpose is not a destination — it's a compass. When you live aligned with it, your steps may not be easy, but they will always be meaningful.

Chapter 23: Integrity & Being Principled — Doing What's Right, Even When It's Hard

"Integrity is doing the right thing, even when no one is watching." –C.S. Lewis

Understanding the Trait

Integrity is when your actions match your values. It's not just about being honest with others — it's about being honest with yourself. It doesn't mean you're flawless or perfect. It means you try to be consistent, even when no one's watching.

> *"Integrity is telling myself the truth. Honesty is telling the truth to other people."*
>
> *– Spencer Johnson*

Living with integrity means listening to your inner compass. It's choosing what's right even when it's not easy, trendy, or rewarded. That's what being principled is: letting your values guide your behavior, not your convenience.

> *"Your actions should reflect your values, not your convenience."*

– *Unknown*

When someone lacks integrity, you'll notice it. They might:

- Say one thing and do another.

- Compromise on values for attention or personal gain.

- Justify questionable behavior under pressure.

- Only "do the right thing" when others are watching

  "It is not what we say or feel that makes us who we are. It is what we do."

  – *Jane Austen*

And truthfully, integrity doesn't demand applause. It just asks you to live in a way you're not ashamed of later.

Why It Matters

Integrity builds self-respect. When you live in alignment with your values, your confidence feels real, not fragile. You trust yourself more — and others can trust you, too.

- You speak with clarity because your words are backed by action.

- You don't have to remember what you said — because it matches what you did.

- You show up as dependable in a world where that's rare.

> *"In matters of style, swim with the current; in matters of principle, stand like a rock."*
>
> *— Thomas Jefferson*

Be flexible where it doesn't matter — but firm where it does. Your principles aren't negotiable.

> *"You can't have a good day with a bad attitude, and you can't have a good life without integrity."*
>
> *— Zig Ziglar*

Integrity also protects your peace. When you go against your values, you may gain something short term — attention, success, approval — but you lose something internal. And that's not worth it.

> *"Success will come and go, but integrity is forever."*
>
> *— Amy Rees Anderson*

How to Cultivate It (Step-by-Step)

Step 1: Know What You Stand For

If you don't know what your values are, how can you live by them?

Ask yourself:

- What qualities do I admire most in others?

- What moments make me feel proud of who I am?

- What kind of person do I want to be when no one is watching?

Write down 3–5 values that really matter to you. Keep them somewhere visible.

Step 2: Match Your Words With Your Actions

If you say it, follow through

- If you promise something, show up.

- If you say you value honesty, be honest — even when it's uncomfortable.

- If you believe in kindness, don't gossip behind someone's back.

  "Honor your word, even when it's uncomfortable."

  – Unknown

Step 3: Choose What's Right, Even if It's Hard

Integrity costs something. Time. Comfort. Popularity. But it's always worth it.

Ask yourself:

- Would I still make this choice if no one knew about it?

- Would I feel proud telling this story to my younger self?

> *"Right is right, even if no one is doing it; wrong is wrong, even if everyone is doing it."*
>
> *— Augustine of Hippo*

> *"Stand for what's right, even if you stand alone."*
>
> *— Unknown*

Do the right thing, even if no one claps.

Step 4: Set Boundaries That Reflect Your Values

Sometimes living by your principles means saying no — and disappointing people. That's okay.

- Don't overexplain.

- Don't shrink.

- Let your boundaries speak for what you believe in

Step 5: Own It When You Mess Up

Living with integrity doesn't mean never slipping — it means owning your slipups.

- Admit it.

- Apologize if needed.

- Make it right.

- Move forward a little wiser.

  "To live with integrity is to be at peace with your reflection."

  — Unknown

Try This Today

Think of one area in your life where you know you've compromised a little — maybe to please someone, avoid conflict, or take the easy road.
Now ask yourself:

- What would the principled version of me choose instead?

- What's one small step I can take today to realign with that?

Do that. Quietly. No need to announce it. Let your integrity speak for itself.

Reflection Prompts

- What values do I hold most dearly — and am I living by them every day?

- When do I tend to act out of convenience instead of principle?

- Have I ever chosen silence over speaking up for what's right?

- In what ways can I become more consistent between my beliefs and my behavior?

- What does "doing the right thing" look like in my life right now

Final Thought to Remember

When the noise fades and the world quiets down, what's left isn't what you gained — it's how you lived.
Live in a way you're proud to remember. That's integrity.

Chapter 24: Authenticity — Being Real Over Being Perfect

"Be yourself; everyone else is already taken." — *Oscar Wilde*

Understanding the Trait

Authenticity is the courage to show up as you are — without masks, filters, or performance. It's the decision to be **genuine** instead of **flawless**, **honest** instead of **pleasing**, and **real** instead of **ideal**.

In a world that celebrates appearances and perfection, being authentic is a quiet way of choosing honesty over image.

Authenticity doesn't mean sharing everything or being blunt without compassion. It means being internally aligned — where your words, actions, and values reflect who you truly are.

People who struggle with authenticity often:

- Hide parts of themselves out of fear of judgment

- Constantly adjust their personality to fit others' expectations

- Strive to appear "together" even when they feel lost

- Confuse acceptance with approval

  "When you show up authentic, you create the space for others to do the same. Walk in your truth."

  – Unknown

Authenticity is not about being flawless. It's about being **honest with yourself** and **brave enough to live it**.

Why It Matters

When you're not authentic, you're not living your life — you're performing it. And performance, no matter how convincing, is exhausting.

Pretending to be someone you're not creates:

- Inner conflict and emotional fatigue

- Superficial connections with others

- Chronic self-doubt, imposter syndrome, and anxiety

- A disconnection from your own desires, limits, and values

  "The privilege of a lifetime is to become who you truly are."

— *Carl Jung*

When you embrace authenticity:

- You stop living for applause and start living for alignment

- Your relationships deepen

- Your inner critic quiets down — because there's no act to maintain

- You begin to trust your voice, your pace, and your values

  "Authenticity is the daily practice of letting go of who we think we're supposed to be and embracing who we are."

  — *Brené Brown*

Authenticity is freedom — not from imperfection, but from pretense.

How to Cultivate It (Step-by-Step)

Step 1: Identify the Masks You Wear

Ask yourself:

- "Where in life do I feel I can't be fully myself?"

- "Who do I shrink for, or pretend around?"

182

- "What am I afraid people would reject if they saw it?"

Awareness is the first act of authenticity.

Step 2: Practice Small Acts of Realness

Start by being honest in low-risk situations:

- Say "no" when you mean it

- Express what you actually think (respectfully)

- Share something personal without fear of appearing imperfect

  "Honesty and transparency make you vulnerable. Be honest and transparent anyway."

  — Mother Teresa

Step 3: Align With Your Values

Authenticity isn't just emotional — it's moral.
Ask:

- *"What matters most to me?"*

- *"Am I living in alignment with what I believe in?"*

- *"What decisions or compromises make me feel fake?"*

You don't have to explain your truth. But you do need to live by it.

Step 4: Stop Apologizing for Who You Are

You are allowed to have flaws.
You are allowed to outgrow people and spaces.
You are allowed to be both a work in progress and deeply worthy.

Step 5: Surround Yourself With Safe People

Authenticity is hard to sustain in unsafe environments. Seek spaces and relationships where your realness is met with respect, not resistance.

You'll know you're in the right space when you no longer feel the need to shrink.

Try This Today

Think of one moment where you felt like you were performing or pretending.
Then ask:

- What part of me was I trying to hide?

- What fear was I trying to avoid?

- What would it look like to be just a little more real next time?

Then — take one small action that feels more true.

Reflection Prompts

- What version of myself do I present to others, and why?

- Where do I feel safest being authentic — and what makes it safe?

- Have I ever betrayed my values to be liked or accepted?

- What does it mean to live a life that's real — not perfect?

- How would I live differently if I trusted that being myself was enough?

Final Thought to Remember

Authenticity is not about proving yourself. It's about returning to yourself — and realizing you were enough all along.

Chapter 25: Self Motivation & Inner Drive — Fueling Progress from Within

"Motivation gets you going, but discipline keeps you growing." – John C. Maxwell

Understanding the Trait

Self-motivation is the ability to take initiative without needing external rewards, pressure, or validation. It's the inner voice that urges you to move forward — not because someone is watching, but because *you* care.

Inner drive is the consistent force behind that motivation. It's the deep-rooted energy that keeps you going, even when things are slow, difficult, or unclear.

> *"Self-motivation is the spark, but discipline is the engine."*
>
> *– Unknown*

People who rely solely on external motivation often:

- Burn out when praise or recognition fades

- Lose consistency during quiet seasons

- Start strong but fail to finish

- Feel helpless when results don't show up quickly

Self-motivation isn't about hype or hustle — it's about having a *why* that matters enough to carry you forward even in silence.

Why It Matters

Self-motivation is the fuel that sustains progress.
It helps you show up, not just when you feel inspired, but when you've committed to growth — even when no one else sees the effort.

With strong inner drive, you:

- Become less dependent on praise or validation

- Build long-term momentum

- Persevere through resistance and uncertainty

- Stay focused on purpose, not just productivity

  "When you feel like quitting,
  remember why you started."

  – Unknown

Motivation may fluctuate. But when your drive is internal, your foundation is stronger than your feelings.

  "You don't need a loud voice to make
  a powerful move. You just need a

*quiet decision followed by steady
steps."*

— Unknown

How to Cultivate It (Step-by-Step)

Step 1: Know Your Inner "Why"

Surface-level goals won't fuel you for long. Dig deeper.
Ask:

- "Why does this matter to me — really?"

- "What would it mean if I gave up on this?

Attach your goals to something personal, meaningful, and
deep.

*"If you only work when you're
motivated, you'll never be
consistent."*

— Mel Robbins

Step 2: Set Small, Daily Commitments

Progress builds motivation.
Instead of waiting for motivation to begin, begin small to
build momentum.

Try:

- "Today, I'll show up for 10 minutes."

- "I'll finish one meaningful task not ten." —

  "Success doesn't come from what you do occasionally. It comes from what you do consistently."

  — Marie Forleo

Step 3: Celebrate Effort, Not Just Outcomes

Waiting for results can drain your drive.
Instead, learn to value effort — the showing up, the learning, the resilience.

Say to yourself:

- *"I'm proud of how I stayed focused today."*

- *"Even slow steps matter."*

Step 4: Use Discipline to Reinforce Motivation

Motivation gets you started. Discipline keeps you going.

When motivation fades:

- Show up out of commitment

- Stay focused on your values, not your mood

- Use structure to support your consistency

  "Discipline is remembering what you want."

189

Try This Today

Write down one area where you've felt unmotivated lately. Now ask:

- *"What's one meaningful reason to continue?"*

- *"What is one small action I can take today — even if it's imperfect?"*

Do it — not because you feel like it, but because you said you would.

> **"Do it because it aligns with who you are becoming — not just because you feel like it."**
>
> *– Unknown*

Reflection Prompts

- What usually motivates me — external praise or internal purpose?

- What goals or habits feel tied to my deepest values?

- What drains my motivation, and how can I work around it?

- When have I surprised myself by pushing through when no one was watching?

- What does "self-driven" look like for me on a daily basis?

Final Thought to Remember

You don't need to wait for motivation to arrive. You can create it — with one meaningful reason and one small, determined step at a time.

Chapter 26: Self Confidence & Assertiveness — Owning Your Worth and Speaking It Clearly

"Confidence is not 'they will like me.' Confidence is 'I'll be fine if they don't.'" – Christina Grimmie

Understanding the Trait

Self-confidence is the belief in your own worth, abilities, and value — not in comparison to others, but in alignment with your truth. Assertiveness is the ability to express that truth clearly, respectfully, and without fear.

True confidence doesn't mean being loud, bold, or always certain.
It means being **grounded in who you are**, even in uncertain situations.
And assertiveness doesn't mean aggression — it's the calm strength to speak up, set boundaries, and communicate clearly.

> *"Confidence is silent. Insecurities are loud."*
>
> *– Unknown*

192

Loudness is not a measure of confidence — often, it's a cover for insecurity. Real confidence doesn't need to prove itself.

> *"An empty vessel makes the loudest sound."*
>
> *– Plato*

Self-confidence that is rooted internally is enduring — it's steady even when opinions shift, praise fades, or challenges arise. Confidence that depends on external validation, however, often leads to comparison, self-doubt, and people pleasing.

> *"If your confidence is built on applause, it will crumble in silence."*
>
> *– Unknown*

Why It Matters

When you develop confidence from within, you become:

- More resilient to criticism

- Less dependent on approval

- Clearer in your decisions

- More capable of speaking honestly, without apology

  > *"Self-confidence is the best outfit."*
  >
  > *– Unknown*

And when you learn to be assertive, you:

- Express your needs without guilt

- Protect your time and energy

- Gain respect

- Build more honest relationships

Assertiveness empowers you to communicate your thoughts without shrinking or over-explaining.
It creates clarity — not confusion. Respect — not resentment.

> *"Your words shape your identity —*
> *speak with the tone of someone who*
> *knows they matter."*
>
> *– Unknown*

How to Cultivate It (Step-by-Step)

Step 1: Build Confidence From the Inside Out

Ask yourself:

- *"What do I like about who I am — beyond what I do?"*

- *"What have I overcome or learned that makes me strong?"*

Confidence isn't about perfection — it's about self-respect.

"True confidence is not thinking you're better than others — it's knowing you don't have to compare yourself at all."

— Unknown

Step 2: Stop Sourcing Your Worth Externally

Validation can feel good, but don't build your identity on it.

Affirm:

- "My worth isn't up for negotiation."

- "Even without applause, I am enough."

  "When you accept yourself, you free yourself from the need to prove yourself."

  — Unknown

Step 3: Practice Assertive Communication

Assertiveness isn't about control — it's about clarity.

Try using:

- "*I feel...*" instead of blaming

- "*I prefer...*" instead of apologizing "*No, thank you.*" without justification

You can be kind and firm at the same time.

> *"Speak the truth, even if your voice shakes."*
>
> *– Maggie Kuhn*

Step 4: Watch Your Body Language

Your posture often speaks before your words.
Stand tall, breathe evenly, make eye contact — these subtle signals reinforce inner belief.

> *"Your body language is your first voice."*
>
> *– Unknown*

Step 5: Celebrate Progress, Not Perfection

Confidence grows through action. Every time you speak up, hold a boundary, or trust yourself — you're strengthening your foundation.

Try This Today

Reflect on a recent moment when you stayed silent or unsure.
Now write down what you could have said.

Then practice one assertive statement today: a boundary, a need, or an honest opinion — calmly and clearly.

Reflection Prompts

- Do I believe I'm worthy, even when I'm not praised or validated?

- When do I shrink myself to avoid disapproval or discomfort?

- Do I communicate my needs clearly — or hint and hope?

- Where have I already shown courage that I've overlooked?

- What would it feel like to speak with quiet, calm confidence?

Final Thought to Remember

You don't need to be the loudest in the room to be heard.
When your confidence is real and your voice is clear, you speak with power — even in silence.

Chapter 27: Positive Mindset — Choosing Perspective Over Negativity

"As you think, so shall you become." – Bruce Lee

Understanding the Trait

A positive mindset is not about pretending everything is perfect — it's about choosing how you respond to what's imperfect. It's the ability to see challenges as temporary, setbacks as lessons, and the future as open to growth.

Positivity doesn't mean ignoring pain. It means refusing to let pain define your attitude.

> *"Positive thinking is not about expecting the best to happen every time, but accepting that whatever happens is the best for this moment."*
>
> *— Unknown*

A negative mindset, on the other hand, filters the world through fear, doubt, and criticism. It assumes the worst, expects failure, and often projects inner struggles onto others.

We truly are a product of our thoughts.
The thoughts we repeat shape our perspective, emotions, and

ultimately our behavior. The more we choose empowering, hopeful, or grateful thoughts, the more our reality shifts to reflect them.

> *"Your life is as good as your mindset."*
>
> *—Unknown*

Negativity isn't just a mood — it's a mental habit. And like any habit, it can be unlearned.

Why It Matters

Your mindset shapes your emotional world, your relationships, and even your outcomes.
Your thoughts become your self-talk, your self-talk shapes your choices, and your choices shape your life.

A positive mindset helps you:

- Cope better with stress

- Build emotional resilience

- Form stronger relationships

- Approach life with hope and energy

  > *"Happiness is not the absence of problems, it's the ability to deal with them."*

When you shift from a reactive mindset to a reflective one, you reclaim control over your outlook — and your outcomes.

> *"You can't always choose your circumstances, but you can always choose your lens."*

– *Unknown*

How to Cultivate It (Step-by-Step)

Step 1: Become Aware of Your Thought Patterns

Pay attention to how you speak to yourself and others. Ask:

- *"Am I assuming the worst?"*

- *"Do I look for problems more than possibilities?"*

Awareness is the first step in changing the story you're telling yourself.

Step 2: Interrupt the Inner Critic

Negative thoughts thrive when left unchecked.

When you catch your inner critic, gently challenge it:

- "Is this thought absolutely true?"

- "Would I say this to someone I love & admire?"

Replace harshness with understanding — even in your inner world.

> *"Talk to yourself like someone you love."*
>
> *– Brené Brown*

Step 3: Shift From Complaints to Gratitude

For every complaint, practice finding one thing you're thankful for.

This doesn't mean denying the problem — it means seeing the bigger picture.

> *"Gratitude unlocks the fullness of life."*
>
> *– Melody Beattie*

Step 4: Reframe Challenges as Lessons

A positive mindset doesn't deny difficulty — it transforms how you relate to it.
Ask:

- *"What is this teaching me?"*

- *"How might I grow through this?"*

  "Every setback is a setup for a comeback."

Step 5: Surround Yourself With Positivity

The people, content, and environments around you influence your thoughts.

Choose wisely:

- Spend time with uplifting voices

- Limit toxic influences

- Consume content that inspires instead of drains

Try This Today

Write down one recurring negative thought you tend to believe.
Now reframe it by writing a kinder, more constructive version of that same thought.

For Example:
"I always mess things up." → "I've made mistakes, but I'm learning and improving."

Reflection Prompts

- What kind of thoughts fill my mind on a daily basis?

- How do my thoughts affect the way I speak and act?

- What beliefs about myself or life might be holding me back?

- In what ways am I already more positive than I used to be?

- What mindset shift would change how I show up tomorrow?

Final Thought to Remember

You don't need to be blindly optimistic — just consciously intentional.
A positive mindset isn't about denying reality. It's about choosing the lens that helps you grow through it.

Chapter 28: Self Acceptance & Self-Respect — Honoring Who You Are, As You Are

"You alone are enough. You have nothing to prove to anybody." — Maya Angelou

Understanding the Trait

Self-acceptance is the willingness to embrace yourself as you are — not just the polished parts, but the flaws, the struggles, and the unfinished pieces.
It is the quiet confidence that says: *I may not be perfect, but I am still worthy.*

Self respect is the natural outcome of self-acceptance.
It is the internal standard that says: *I deserve to be treated with dignity — by others and by myself.*

> *"The curious paradox is that when I accept myself just as I am, then I can change."*
>
> *– Carl Rogers*

Self-respect is rooted in dignity and boundaries. Arrogance is rooted in superiority and ego.

People who struggle with self acceptance often:

- Criticize themselves constantly

- Feel unworthy unless they're achieving or pleasing

- Compare their flaws to others' strengths

- Apologize for existing or taking up space

- Mistake self-respect for arrogance

Without self-acceptance, even success feels hollow — because you're building your life on the belief that you're not enough.

Why It Matters

When you accept yourself, you stop fighting with yourself. You stop resisting your own flaws and begin to live in peace with who you are.

Self Acceptance gives you:

- Freedom from the pressure to be perfect

- Permission to grow without shame

- Inner safety to explore, fail, and try again

- The clarity to protect your peace through boundaries

> *"To be beautiful means to be yourself. You don't need to be accepted by others. You need to accept yourself."*

Self-respect builds on this foundation.
 It sets the tone for how others treat you — and how you treat yourself.

When you lack self-respect, you:

- Tolerate what hurts you

- Say "yes" when you mean "no"

- Let guilt pressure you into violating your own values

- Diminish your own voice

  "Respect yourself enough to walk away from anything that no longer serves you, grows you, or makes you happy."

  — Robert Tew

Self-acceptance heals your relationship with yourself. Self-respect protects it.

How to Cultivate It (Step-by-Step)

Step 1: Let Go of the Belief That You Must Earn Your Worth

Ask yourself:

- *"What makes me believe I have to 'deserve' love or respect first?"*

- *"Who taught me that I had to be different to be enough?"*

- *"What if I stopped chasing worth and chose to stand in it instead?"*

Your worth is not a reward. It's your starting point.

Step 2: Speak to Yourself Like Someone You Love

Would you speak to a friend the way you speak to yourself?

Replace criticism with compassion:

- "I messed up" becomes "I'm learning."

- "I'm not enough" becomes "I'm still growing."

- "I hate this part of me" becomes "This part of me needs love."

Step 3: Respect Your Boundaries and Values

You show yourself respect when you:

- Say "no" without guilt

- Stand up for your needs

- Honor your time, energy, and space

- Stay true to what matters to you

Self-respect is not selfish. It's self-preserving.

Step 4: Stop Apologizing for Who You Are

You don't have to shrink to make others comfortable
You don't need to apologize for who you are.

> *"Never bend your head. Always hold
> it high. Look the world straight in the
> eye."*
>
> *– Helen Keller*

Step 5: Allow Yourself to Be Both a Work in Progress and Already Worthy

You can accept yourself without staying stuck.
You can improve your life while still honoring who you are right now.

You don't have to be perfect to be respected.
You just have to be honest, kind, and real.

Try This Today

Write down five things you appreciate about yourself — not for what you've accomplished, but for simply being you.

Reflection Prompts

- In what ways do I attach my worth to achievement or appearance?

- How do I speak to myself when I make a mistake?

- Where in my life do I let others treat me in ways I wouldn't accept from myself?

- What would change if I truly respected my time, energy, and values?

- What would it look like to accept myself without needing to change first?

Final Thought to Remember

Self-acceptance is the soil.
Self-respect is the boundary.
Together, they create the space where your true self can grow freely.

Chapter 29: Self Discipline & Self Control — Leading Yourself with Purpose, Not Pressure

"Discipline is the bridge between goals and accomplishment." – Jim Rohn

Understanding the Trait

Self-discipline is the ability to stay committed to your values and goals, even when motivation fades. It's doing what needs to be done — not just when you feel like it, but because you know it matters.

Self-control is the ability to pause, resist, or redirect impulses when they conflict with your long-term values. It's the space between urge and action — the muscle that helps you respond, not react.

> *"What you do every day matters more than what you do once in a while."*
>
> *– Gretchen Rubin*

Together, self-discipline and self-control form the foundation of consistency. Without them, dreams remain intentions. With them, progress becomes possible.

People who lack these traits often:

- Start things but rarely finish

- Give in to distractions or emotional impulses

- Depend on external pressure or fear to take action

- Feel like life controls them instead of the other way around

Self-discipline is not punishment. Self-control is not suppression. Both are forms of inner leadership — guiding yourself with strength, clarity, and grace.

Why It Matters

You can't control the world. But you can learn to control yourself — your choices, your habits, your attitude.

Self-discipline builds trust with yourself:

- You become someone who follows through

- You build momentum even on hard days

- You gain quiet confidence that doesn't rely on hype

Self-control protects you from emotional sabotage:

- It gives you space to respond wisely instead of reacting impulsively

- It helps you walk away from what isn't aligned — even if it's tempting

- It allows you to maintain your values in moments of stress or chaos

"He who conquers himself is the mightiest warrior."

— Confucius

Discipline moves you forward.
Control keeps you aligned.
Together, they turn intention into integrity.

How to Cultivate It (Step-by-Step)

Step 1: Know What You're Serving

Discipline and control are hard to sustain if you're unsure about *why* they both matter.

Ask yourself:

- *"What kind of individual do I want to become?"*

- *"What values am I committed to — even when it's uncomfortable?"*

- *"What's the cost of giving in to every urge?"*

Your "why" gives your habits meaning.

Step 2: Make Structure Support, Not Squeeze You

Discipline thrives in clarity, not rigidity.
Create routines that work with your nature — not against it.

Examples:

- Block time for focused work, but allow breathing room

- Replace "I have to" with "I get to"

- Use reminders, not shame, to stay on track

  "Motivation gets you started. Habit keeps you going."

  – Jim Ryun

Step 3: Learn to Pause Before Giving In

Practice the art of pause:

- Take 5 deep breaths before reacting emotionally

- Wait 10 minutes before checking your phone

- Choose one thing to finish before starting another

These moments build internal strength over time.

Step 4: Keep Commitments to Yourself

Start small — and follow through:

- "I will wake up when I said I would."

- "I will honor this one healthy meal."

- "I will say no when I mean no."

  "Success is nothing more than a few simple disciplines practiced every day."

  – Jim Rohn

Each act of follow-through deepens your self-respect.

Step 5: Forgive Slip-Ups, But Don't Excuse Them

Self-discipline requires grace, not guilt.
Missing a day isn't failure — giving up on yourself is.

If you slip:

- Acknowledge it honestly

- Reconnect with your purpose

- Begin again — without the baggage

Try This Today

Choose one small area where you've been inconsistent — waking up, drinking water, staying focused, managing your mood.

Then ask:

- What's the tiniest next step I can follow through on today?

- How can I make it easier, not harder?

Follow through. Just once. Then do it again tomorrow.

Reflection Prompts

- Where in my life right now, do I need self-discipline the most?

- What patterns do I fall into when I lack self-control?

- What helps me stay focused even when motivation is low?

- What's one habit I'm proud of having built — and how did I do it?

Final Thought to Remember

Self-discipline is not about forcing yourself. It's about choosing yourself — again and again — with clarity, purpose, and strength.

Chapter 30: Mindfulness & Presence — Living Fully in the Now

"The present moment is the only time over which we have dominion." – Thích Nhất Hạnh

Understanding the Trait

Mindfulness is the practice of intentionally bringing your attention to the present moment — without judgment, distraction, or resistance. It's not about controlling your thoughts, but learning to notice them without being controlled by them.

Presence is the state of being *fully here* — physically, mentally, and emotionally. It's listening without wandering, breathing without rushing, and doing without splitting your focus between what is and what might be.

> *"Mindfulness isn't difficult, we just need to remember to do it."*
>
> *– Sharon Salzberg*

Although mindfulness and self-awareness are closely related, they serve different purposes.
Self-awareness is reflective — it's about understanding yourself: your patterns, your reactions,

your deeper motives.

Mindfulness is experiential — it's about being with yourself in the moment, engaging life as it unfolds.

When we lack mindfulness, we live on autopilot:

- Thinking about what happened or what could happen

- Reacting impulsively rather than responding intentionally

- Multitasking our way through life, but missing it entirely

Mindfulness is not about perfection or peace at all times. It's about awareness — choosing to be awake to life as it unfolds.

Why It Matters

You cannot change the past. You cannot control the future. But the present is always available — and that's where your power lives.

Mindfulness offers:

- Reduced anxiety and rumination

- Greater emotional regulation

- Deeper focus and productivity

- Improved relationships, because presence makes others feel seen

"Wherever you are, be there totally."

– Eckhart Tolle

Presence makes life feel richer, even without more.
It reconnects you to your breath, your surroundings, your body — and to people.
It invites you to slow down, not because you're behind, but because this moment deserves your full attention

"Life is available only in the present moment. If you abandon the present moment, you cannot live the moments of your daily life deeply."

– Thích Nhất Hạnh

How to Cultivate It (Step-by-Step)

Step 1: Pause and Notice

The first step to mindfulness is awareness.
Where is your mind right now? What are you feeling, sensing, or hearing? Try this anytime during the day:

- Notice your breath

- Feel your feet on the ground

- Listen to the sounds around you

Mindfulness begins with a moment of pause.

Step 2: Practice Single-Tasking

Presence thrives when you stop doing many things at once.

Choose one task and do it fully:

- Drink your tea without checking your phone

- Write or type with full focus

- Walk without needing a destination — just notice your steps

Step 3: Anchor Yourself With Breath

Your breath is your ever-present anchor.
When the mind races, return to your breath. No force, no control — just awareness.

Try:

- Breathing in: "I am here"

- Breathing out: "This moment is enough"

Step 4: Respond Instead of React

Mindfulness gives you space between trigger and response.
Before reacting impulsively, ask:

- "What am I really feeling?"

- "What is the wisest way to respond?"

This space is where peace begins.

Try This Today

Pause and do one task slowly — with full attention.
Feel each movement. Breathe with awareness.
Let the moment be enough without needing to rush to the next.

Reflection Prompts

- Where in my day do I tend to rush or live unconsciously?

- What thoughts often pull me out of the present?

- When do I feel most grounded in the now — and what helps me stay there?

- How do I feel when someone is fully present with me? Do I offer that to others?

- What would change if I gave this moment more attention?

Final Thought to Remember

You don't need more time. You need more presence in the time you already have.

Peace, clarity, and connection all begin in the now.

Chapter 31: Resilience — Rising Stronger Through Life's Storms

"Resilience is not about never falling — it's about rising every time you do." — Unknown

Understanding the Trait

Resilience is the inner strength that allows you to bend without breaking, to stumble without staying down, and to keep going even when everything in you feels like giving up. It's not the absence of pain — it's the ability to move through pain with purpose.

Resilience doesn't make life easier — it makes you stronger. It is built in the hard moments, not the easy ones.

> *"You cannot stop the waves, but you can learn to surf."*
>
> *– Jon Kabat-Zinn*

Resilient people aren't immune to adversity. They feel, they struggle, they even fall apart sometimes — but they always come back together.
What sets them apart is their mindset: they view difficulty as part of the path, not the end of it.

"You may have to fight a battle more than once to win it."

— Margaret Thatcher

Why It Matters

Resilience allows you to:

- Adapt to change without losing your identity

- Face hardship without being consumed by it

- Recover from failure with wisdom instead of shame

- Build a life that isn't free from struggle — but full of strength

  "Life doesn't get easier or more forgiving, we get stronger and more resilient."

  — Steve Maraboli

  "It's not the load that breaks you down, it's the way you carry it."

  — Lou Holtz

This means it's not the challenge itself, but how you mentally approach and respond to it that determines your strength.

Without resilience, challenges feel like dead ends.
With it, they become detours — not destinations.

> *"Sometimes when things are falling apart, they may actually be falling into place."*
>
> *– Unknown*

How to Cultivate It (Step-by-Step)

Step 1: Let Yourself Feel — Then Refocus

Resilience doesn't mean suppressing emotions.
Feel what you feel — frustration, grief, anger — but don't let it define your direction.

Ask yourself:

- *"What do I need to process right now?"*

- *"What small step forward can I take once I'm ready?"*

"Feel it fully. Then rise."

Step 2: Learn From Every Fall

Every setback has something to teach — about yourself, about others, about what matters.

Ask yourself:

- *"What did I gain from this experience?"*

- *"How will I do it differently next time?"*

Mistakes don't make you weaker — avoiding the lesson does.

Step 3: Reconnect With Your Inner Strength

Hard moments often make us forget how far we've come.

Remind yourself:

- "I've survived difficulty before."

- "There is strength in me I haven't even fully discovered yet."

Step 4: Focus on What You Can Control

Resilience grows when you stop wasting energy on what's outside your power.

Instead, focus on:

- Your effort

- Your perspective

- Your attitude

- Your next step

  "Start where you are. Use what you have. Do what you can."

  – Arthur Ashe

Step 5: Nourish Your Strength, Don't Just Deplete It

Resilience requires rest and restoration.
You are not a machine. Make time to:

- Reflect

- Recharge

- Rebuild

Rest is not weakness — it's preparation.

Try This Today

Think of a recent hardship or failure you faced.
Now write down:

- What it taught you

- How you showed strength (even if imperfectly)

- **What inner strength you discovered in the process**

Let this reflection remind you: you are more capable than you realize.

Reflection Prompts

- What past difficulty have I overcome that I once thought I couldn't?

- What inner resources did I lean on during tough times?

- Do I judge myself too harshly for struggling?

- How can I shift from "why me?" to "what now?"

- What does resilience look like for me today?

Final Thought to Remember

Resilience isn't about being unbreakable — it's about becoming whole again, no matter how many times you face challenges in life.

Chapter 32: Empathy — Understanding Others Without Losing Yourself

"Empathy is seeing with the eyes of another, listening with the ears of another, and feeling with the heart of another." – Alfred Adler

Understanding the Trait

Empathy is the ability to feel with others — to sense their pain, joy, or fear without judgment. It's not about fixing, rescuing, or agreeing. It's about being present, understanding, and human.

Empathy is a bridge — not a solution. It connects hearts where words may fail.

> *"Empathy is not absorbing others' emotions, it's acknowledging them without becoming them."*
>
> *– Unknown*

True empathy begins with listening — not to respond, but to understand. It's the emotional intelligence to say, *"I may not know your pain, but I honor it."*

At the same time, empathy must be balanced with boundaries.
You can carry understanding without carrying the entire

weight.

You can feel with others without abandoning yourself.

> *"Empathy fuels connection.*
> *Sympathy drives disconnection."*
>
> *– Brené Brown*

Empathy invites us into someone's experience, saying "I'm with you." Sympathy often creates distance by standing apart and saying "I feel sorry for you."

Why It Matters

Empathy builds trust, softens defensiveness, and heals emotional distance.

Without empathy:

- We react instead of respond

- We judge instead of understand

- We create walls instead of bridges

With empathy:

- Relationships deepen

- Conflicts de-escalate

- Compassion becomes part of our character

> *"We think we listen, but very rarely do we listen with real understanding."*
>
> *– Carl Rogers*

Empathy also builds inner maturity — it reminds us that everyone is human, everyone is flawed, and everyone is doing the best they can with what they've been given.

How to Cultivate It (Step-by-Step)

Step 1: Be Present Without a Solution

Resist the urge to fix.
Just *be there*, offer space, not answers.

Say:

- *"That sounds really tough."*

- *"I'm here with you, even if I don't have the words."*

  > *"Sometimes the most healing thing you can do is simply hold space for someone."*
  >
  > *– Unknown*

Step 2: Ask, Don't Assume

You can't truly understand someone unless you ask what their experience feels like to *them*.

Try:

- "How has this been for you?"

- "What do you need most right now?"

Empathy grows not from guessing — but from gently inviting someone to be seen.

Step 3: Listen Between the Lines

People don't always say what they mean. Empathy listens beyond the words — into tone, silence, and energy.

Pay attention to:

- What's said and unsaid

- What's loud and what's missing

- The feeling underneath the facts

Step 4: Know the Difference Between Empathy and Over-Identification

It's one thing to feel with someone. It's another to get consumed by their emotions.

You can be compassionate and grounded at the same time.

Try This Today

Think of someone you've been judging, misunderstanding, or feeling distanced from.

Ask yourself:

- *"What might they be going through that I can't see?"*

- *"How would I want someone to treat me if I were in their place?"*

Then reach out — with kindness, not correction.

Reflection Prompts

- When was the last time I truly listened to someone without interrupting or fixing?

- Do I create space for people to feel safe sharing with me?

- What assumptions do I often make about others that block my empathy?

- How can I balance empathy with emotional boundaries?

Final Thought to Remember

Empathy doesn't require you to have all the answers.
It only asks you to show up with your heart open and

your presence real.
Sometimes, that alone is enough to change everything.

Chapter 33: Gratitude — A Mindset of Appreciation

"Gratitude turns what we have into enough." –
Aesop

Understanding the Trait

Gratitude isn't just about saying "thank you" — it's a way of seeing. It's about choosing to notice what's good, even when things aren't perfect. It shifts your focus from what's missing to what's already meaningful.

It's easy to fall into the habit of always chasing more — more success, more approval, more comfort. But gratitude gently reminds you that what you have, right now, is worth honoring.

> *"Gratitude helps you see what is there instead of what isn't.."*
>
> *– Unknown*

This doesn't mean ignoring pain or pretending life is always bright. It means allowing beauty and difficulty to coexist — and still finding something to be thankful for in the middle of it all.

People who struggle with gratitude often:

- Overlook small joys while waiting for something "big"

- Feel frustrated when things don't go as planned

- Focus more on lack than abundance

- Take daily comforts for granted

On the other hand, gratitude creates a steady sense of contentment — one that doesn't rely on circumstances.

> *"It is not joy that makes us grateful;*
> *it is gratitude that makes us joyful."*
>
> *– David Steindl-Rast*

Why It Matters

Gratitude changes how you experience the world. It doesn't fix every problem, but it gives you a lens that brings clarity and peace. You start to see that even imperfect days carry quiet blessings.

Practicing gratitude can help you:

- Worry less and enjoy more

- Improve your relationships through appreciation

- Feel more grounded and hopeful, even during challenges

- Shift your mindset from "not enough" to "this is plenty"

"Gratitude is a powerful catalyst for happiness. It's the spark that lights a fire of joy in your soul."

– Amy Collette

On a biological level, gratitude can actually reshape how your brain responds to stress. When you train your mind to notice the good, it gets better at finding it — even in hard moments.

"Acknowledging the good that you already have in your life is the foundation for all abundance."

– Eckhart Tolle

How to Cultivate It (Step-by-Step)

Step 1: Start Small

You don't need a huge breakthrough to feel grateful. Start by noticing what's right in front of you — your morning cup of coffee, the sound of laughter, the comfort of a warm bed.

Take a moment to say:

- *"This feels good."*

- *"I'm thankful for this moment."*

The simpler the gratitude, the more deeply it roots itself.

Step 2: Shift Comparison Into Perspective

Comparison often blocks gratitude. Instead of focusing on what others have, look at what you once wished for — and now have.

Ask yourself:

- *"What do I have now that I once prayed or hoped for?"*

- *"What in my life would I miss if it disappeared tomorrow?"*

Gratitude is less about having everything — and more about realizing you already have something valuable

Step 3: Trade Expectation for Appreciation

When we expect something and don't receive it, we feel let down. But when we appreciate what *is*, we open the door to peace.

If you catch yourself thinking "this isn't enough," pause and ask:

- *"What is working right now?"*

- *"What can I still be thankful for?"*

"Gratitude unlocks the fullness of life. It turns denial into acceptance, chaos into order, confusion into clarity."

— Melody Beattie

Step 4: Speak It or Write It Down

Saying *"thank you"* isn't just polite — it's powerful. Gratitude multiplies when expressed.

You might try:

- Writing a few things you're grateful for each night

- Sending a kind message to someone who's helped you

- Saying "thank you" out loud for the small wins

What you acknowledge grows stronger.

Step 5: Find Gratitude in Growth

It's easy to feel thankful when things are going well. But deeper gratitude shows up when you can say, *"It was a tough experience, but it made me stronger."*

Even pain can offer perspective. Even disappointment can build strength. Look for the lesson — not just the comfort.

Try This Today

List three things — big or small — that you're thankful for. Then tell someone something you appreciate about them. See how it shifts your energy.

Reflection Prompts

- What simple pleasures do I overlook in daily life?

- Am I usually focused on what's missing — or what's present?

- When did gratitude help me get through something difficult?

- How can I express more appreciation to those around me?

- What would it feel like to live with more gratitude every day

Final Thought to Remember

Gratitude doesn't wait for life to be perfect. It begins the moment you choose to notice — and honor — what's already here.

Chapter 34: Contentment — Finding Peace in What You Already Have

"Richness is not in the quantity of possessions (that one has); rather, true richness is contentment." – Prophet Muhammad (Peace be upon Him)- Prophet of Islam

Understanding the Trait

Contentment is the quiet strength of being satisfied with what you have, where you are, and who you are — without needing to compare, compete, or constantly crave more. It's not the absence of desire or ambition, but the presence of peace.

Many confuse contentment with complacency. But contentment doesn't mean you stop growing — it means you stop chasing fulfillment in things that can't offer it.

> *"Contentment is not the fulfillment of what you want, but the realization of how much you already have."*
>
> *– Unknown*

A content person can be ambitious without being restless. They appreciate the now, even while moving toward what's next.

On the other hand, discontentment often leads to:

- Chronic dissatisfaction, even in abundance

- Envy, resentment, or unhealthy comparison

- A cycle of "I'll be happy when..." thinking

- Restlessness that steals joy from the present moment

Why It Matters

Without contentment, even success feels empty.
Without contentment, gratitude feels short-lived.
And without contentment, peace remains always one step away.

When you cultivate contentment:

- You stop tying your worth to what you have

- You become more grateful for simple blessings

- You experience more presence, less pressure

- You navigate life with more inner steadiness

> *"Happiness will never come to those who fail to appreciate what they already have."*

> *– Gautama Buddha*

Contentment allows you to grow from a place of fullness — not lack. You're no longer chasing fulfillment, but living from it.

> *"Learn to be happy with what you have while you pursue all that you want."*

> *– Jim Rohn*

How to Cultivate It (Step-by-Step)

Step 1: Shift Your Definition of "Enough"

Contentment begins when you redefine what it means to have "*enough.*"
Ask yourself:

- *"Do I truly need this — or am I chasing an illusion?"*

- *"Am I filling a gap with things that don't satisfy?"*

Many people chase wants without realizing their needs are already met. A powerful mindset shift is this:

"I might not have everything I want, but I have everything I need."

That realization alone can bring peace — and reframe how you define a fulfilled life.

True contentment starts when you realize abundance isn't about accumulation — it's about appreciation.

Step 2: Practice Presence Over Projection

Discontentment often comes from living in the "if only" or "what's next."

Practice anchoring yourself in the present:

- Savor a quiet moment

- Listen fully in conversation

- Enjoy what's here without needing it to be more

  "The secret of contentment is knowing how to enjoy what you have."

  — Unknown

Step 3: Replace Comparison with Gratitude

Comparison blinds you to your own blessings.
Gratitude reveals them.

Next time you feel envy creeping in,
Ask:

- *"What do I have right now that I once prayed for?"*

- *"What is going right — even if it's small?"*

Step 4: Celebrate Simplicity

Not everything you desire is meant to be possessed. Contentment finds richness in the simple, the quiet, the ordinary.

- A good meal

- A walk in fresh air

- A kind word

- A moment of calm

These aren't small — they are the soul's true luxuries.

Step 5: Let Go of "Someday" Thinking

Stop postponing peace for a future condition.
Affirm:

- *"I can be fulfilled now, even as I grow."*

- *"This moment is worthy, even if it's not perfect."*

Try This Today

Write a short list titled:

"Things I Take for Granted That Someone Else Is Praying For."

Let that list bring you back to the present. Let it soften your restlessness.

Reflection Prompts

- What simple things do I overlook that deserve more appreciation?

- Where in my life do I confuse "more" with "better"?

- What have I achieved or received that I rarely pause to acknowledge?

- How can I slow down and savor my life more fully?

- If I had everything I wanted right now — how would I act? Can I act that way today?

Final Thought to Remember

You don't have to wait for everything to be perfect to feel at peace.
Contentment is a decision — to value what's here, even while reaching for more.

The Journey You've Taken

This book has not simply offered lessons — it has invited you into a transformation.

You began by turning inward — learning to pause, reflect, and reconnect with who you are beneath the noise.
You explored your purpose, your principles, and the quiet courage it takes to be real in a world that often rewards performance over authenticity.
You built your own fire — self-motivation, confidence, and the mindset to choose growth over gloom.

But true change doesn't end with insight.
It matures through discipline.
It deepens through presence.
And it's tested through challenge.

You've learned to stand steady in storms, to carry your strength with humility, and to walk forward with clarity — even when the way was uncertain.

And then, you turned outward — toward empathy, gratitude, and the kind of peace that comes not from having more, but from needing less.
You arrived at contentment — not as surrender, but as a grounded, vibrant acceptance of life as it is.

If you've come this far, know this:
You have not just finished a book.
You have started a shift.

A shedding of what no longer fits.
A stepping into what was always waiting within you.

A quieter strength.
A deeper clarity.
A truer you.

Carry it with you.
Live it forward.
And most of all — grow gently, and grow true.

The shift has already begun — and it lives within you now.

THIS SPACE IS YOURS.
RETURN TO IT.
REFLECT.
GROW.

THE STORY CONTINUES — WITHIN YOU.

Share Your Thoughts!

If *Inner Clarity* spoke to you in any way, your review can help others discover the message it carries.
Please take a moment to leave a short, honest review on Amazon.
Simply scan the QR code below to go directly to the review page.

Your feedback truly matters — and helps this book reach the readers who need it most.

With appreciation,
David River

www.ingramcontent.com/pod-product-compliance
Lightning Source LLC
Chambersburg PA
CBHW061610120626
46550CB00004B/1679